LANDSCAPE
OF
MOTHERS

Nature Archetypes as a
Guide to Mothering

BY JILL DONEEN CLIFTON

© 2020 Jill Doneen Clifton

Made in the USA

First Edition

ISBN: 978-1-7350726-1-6

Cover Illustration: Olivia Taylor
www.oliviataylorart.com

Cover & Layout Design: Heather Dakota
www.heatherdakota.com

Wyrd & Wyld Publishing
Spokane, WA

Learn more about Landscape of Mothers at:
www.landscapeofmothers.com

For Phoebe, Nora, and Emily

TABLE OF CONTENTS

Part 2: Working with Landscape of Mothers

FOREWORD

When Jill first told me about the writing and development of *Landscape of Mothers*, I felt an electric jolt go down my back. It was not that she was creating the Mothers out of thin air but revealing them to us, interpreting and channeling their wisdom. When I feel that electric surge, I know something powerful and true is happening! With Jill's tending and love, Landscape of Mothers come to us each from their own element when we feel out of or lost within our own. Landscape of Mothers is nothing short of a pithy masterpiece and field guide to the terrains of the soul.

During the writing and birthing of Landscape of Mothers, Jill shared various insights and wisdom from the Mothers with me. There were several times over this period, that I would find myself in the shower (where I do my best thinking) wondering what this Mother would say or what another Mother would ask of me. I so looked forward to checking in and hearing the latest from Jill as the wisdom of the Mothers is so simple in its truth, clear in its guidance, and so deeply potent and effective.

One of my favorite things about Jill (and there are many!) is her love for and inherent understanding of Biomimicry, our looking to nature for solutions to human needs. While Biomimicry is most often used in design, architecture, and for environmental solutions, Jill shares my passion for and brilliantly turns to nature for the challenges of the human spirit and journey. Enter The Landscape of Mothers.

Jill's deep understanding of the natural world has forged a sharp vision into the ever-present but often unseen wisdom and teachings available to us. The

Mothers tend our human nature and the wisdom of the natural world for the ever-evolving landscape of our lives. Individually, each Mother holds (and shares) her own wisdom but together they remind us we need the collective to find our way.

The Landscape of Mothers is relevant to all seasons and landscapes of our lives. They help us see ourselves when we are often in the fog of our own struggle and reorient us in their wisdom and ground us back into ourselves. With solid footing and their compassionate compass, they meet us on each path with the simply profound guidance we need.

Jill could have written thesis upon thesis, and dissertations with insights, analysis, and research that would impact any area of her interest. What she has given us with The Landscape of Mothers to me, offers much, much more. She has given us the vision to see the wisdom available to us and the language and tools to apply it so that we may traverse our own journey. With your reading and actively bringing the Mothers into your life, the book becomes far more powerful and has greater impact than academic publication.

The Landscape of Mothers are the mothers we long for. They allow us to lean into their wisdom when we're not so sure of our own. And like Jill, they are good medicine. This book is one that will live on a bedside table, with earmarked pages, and absorbed spills of tea and coffee, and shared in heart-to-hearts among dear friends.

I hope you discover the Mothers you need in this book. Like me, you will also discover Jill's deep ecology and a mirror that reflects your truth, interconnectedness, and that even in the greatest of challenges, that we are never alone. We have Jill and all the Mothers believing in and championing us along the way.

With gratitude,

Randi Buckley
Mentor, coach, and creator of Healthy Boundaries for Kind People

PREFACE

Welcome to Landscape of Mothers!

I wished for this book when I was a new mother. I knew I wanted to do things differently than my parents did, but I didn't really know what that meant. When I turned to the parenting guidebooks, they told me what to do, but I couldn't be the parent I wanted to be because I didn't have the self-soothing skills or the experience of attachment I needed. *Landscape of Mothers* is a map of my travels to become the kind of parent that I want to be.

Landscape of Mothers is a map of the places I had to go in my inner world to reclaim my Self inside my role of mother. The landscapes are the map locations: sun and moon, wind, desert, island, mountain, river, forest, and ocean. Each location has a gift that is important for mothering. For instance, Wind Mother has the gift of trust, Forest Mother's gift is belonging, and River Mother's gift is purpose. Just like when you take a trip, Landscape of Mothers offers a directory of possibilities, but doesn't determine your experience. There are "itineraries" to choose from, but the experience is your own to create.

In this book, when I talk about mothering, I do not mean "what women do with children." I mean the actions we all take toward creating a culture of care over control, of mutual wellbeing over dominance, and doing whatever it takes to be both inclusive and unique. I mean perceiving children not as property, but as small humans who have the job of finding out and expressing who they truly are.

What if we didn't apply gender stereotypes to mothering? What if, instead we saw it as a verb? What if mothering is an action that we can all participate in regardless of gender identity?

Since I'm talking about mothering as a genderless activity, this book is as relevant to men as it is to women. That means, if you don't identify as a woman and you're wondering if this book is for you... it is. If you don't have kids, but you are working with children or are working toward a culture of care, can this book help? Yes.

Then why is this called Landscape of Mothers? Because it was through my acts of mothering that I learned about what I have written here. Once I had children, I felt the long line of mothers that had come before me. I could see the skills (or lack thereof) that created wounds in my family line that had never been healed. This awareness helped me tend the personal work that was needed, as well as to locate parenting skills I was lacking. I began to ask myself who I needed to become so that I didn't perpetuate more harm.

So, Landscape of Mothers is for people who want to parent differently with the intention of breaking old family patterns of abandonment, neglect, and pain. To do this, we have to embrace different ways of relating. This journey may include addressing old wounds, personal growth work, and cultivating life-affirming ways of being together. Thank you for being one who does this kind of work. Your work toward creating a culture of care is important and appreciated in the world.

One more thing before we start... Each Landscape Mother begins with two quotes that come from moments that I received guidance from that Mother. One quote is in the form of a statement, the other is a *Dekaaz*. *Dekaaz* is a poetic form created by one of my teachers, Rachel Bagby, that encourages the distillation of wisdom into 10 syllable verses, 2/3/5, spoken aloud to another human being. The beauty is not only in the rhythm, but in the form and requirement of birthing each poem out loud. This is important because the act of speaking invites our bodies into the experience of the words, locating deeper understanding and experience. Sometimes, the middle line holds a new perspective or understanding of the poem when held in its own light and cadence. The *Dekaaz* here were written by me and inspired by the essence of each of the Landscape Mothers. I hope they serve as small piece of wisdom you can carry with you.

Part I: The Mothers

INTRODUCTION TO
LANDSCAPE OF MOTHERS

Much of the world seems to be reduced to a dichotomy of good and bad, right and wrong. While some things fall nicely into those categories, most don't. The most meaningful parts of our lives—our relationships, past experiences, and current events—won't allow themselves to be easily placed into such tight boxes.

We could have a long discussion about good and bad, and what all of that even means. But my point here is that good and bad are usually a matter of opinion. People, events, and ways of living are not inherently good or bad. Finding a more constructive way to explore something as complex as motherhood is, ultimately, more helpful.

Landscape of Mothers is about the movement out of the realm of good and bad, and into something with more wholeness, nuance, and expanded possibility. While this discussion isn't only pertinent to motherhood, or even parenthood, it was as a mother that I found my entry to a new world around the limitations of good-versus-bad thinking, and a new awareness of how a shift in perspective could ease some of the tensions that contributed to my suffering.

There was a time I realized that I had experienced about every kind of "being a mother" that one could be in this single lifetime. I was a parentified child, which meant that I took a parenting role in my family often, even when I was very young. I placed a baby for adoption at 18, then I experienced miscarriage and secondary infertility. I went through in vitro fertilization (IVF) treatments, and then I had a surprise baby. I experienced debilitating postpartum depression after my last child, and found myself deeply questioning what it is to be a mother. What makes a good one? Am I a good one? Is there such a thing as a good mother?

In 2015/16, I participated in a program in my local area called The Yoniverse Monologues. I gathered with nine other women for six months, under the guidance of a master storyteller, to craft our stories of being women. Each woman whittled a pivotal piece of her life story into seven powerful minutes, stories we told on stage. We shared, cried, delved deep, and found the core of our stories together. In the crafting of that story I found my inner Council of Mothers. I realized that they were how I survived my journey through motherhood, and I eventually found my true self amongst the hall of mirrors of my depression.

Over the subsequent years, in my continued personal journey and working with other women through this process of reclaiming our Selves amidst motherhood, I've realized that it's not just the Council of Mothers, but that there are other mother archetypes that are part of our inner landscape. As I write this, I stand at another crossroads in my life. One where I have found a sense of place within myself from which I can organize my wanderings and explorations. My hope is that in reading through these archetypes you will be able to see yourself and a little bit about where you are standing. I hope that you will be able to see where you want to go, and that you will be able to orient yourself with the help of the archetypes in the Landscape of Mothers.

These archetypes are written as possible descriptors of the landscape-of-you in your role as mother (to your children, your projects, and yourself). These are the archetypes that I have known most intimately and felt capable of naming. There are many more that I have not written about here. Don't hesitate to write your own. You will know parts of Mother that I do not. And it is in the collection of stories in community that we will know the full range of what it is to be a mother. And then all women will know our choices, and we will be able to claim our autonomy within our mothering.

I write the Mothers from the perspective that they are facets of each of us. When we take a part of ourselves, back up from it a bit, name it, and really look at it, we might find things we couldn't see when we were inside of it. Archetypes afford us the possibility of taking a part of us that is intricately embedded inside of the whole of who we are, stepping back from it, and investigating it. Although it's an artificial separation to perceive a part in isolation, the perspective offered can be enlightening. Hopefully, we see something about ourselves anew, with increased understanding, compassion, clarity, or some other insight. We can pull this new awareness in close again, now better able to utilize the skills and knowledge. That is, we will be better able to know our own capacities and use them with intention and awareness.

When we want to parent in a way that is more aware, kind, loving, caring, boundaried, value-driven, or life-affirming than how we were raised, we are in something of a bind. We don't want to be the kind of parent we grew up with, but what are we supposed to do? There are two big hurdles to overcome.

One hurdle is obvious. If we grew up with parents we don't want to emulate, we don't have a model for the kind of parent we want to be. We don't have the unwritten "playbook." We don't have an image in our minds of what this different kind of parenting would look like. So, we tend to pick up parenting books in the hopes that we can figure that out as adults.

Secondly, there's something else we're missing that isn't acknowledged in those parenting advice books. We often didn't get the skills that are needed to be the kind of parent presented in the books. There are instructions on what to do with a screaming toddler, but it is assumed that we have the internal self-mastery required to actually do it. The parenting books tell us *what to do*, but not *how to be*. To parent well you need skills and competencies that you may never have learned in your family of origin.

How do you do what you never learned? How do you embody and represent values you never saw embodied and represented that you want to bring forward in your parenting? The authors of parenting books tell you how to act and what to say, but they don't really tell you how to be truly present. They assume you have skills of self-soothing, deep listening, nervous system regulation, and secure attachment. To have these skills, there's some repair work to do, some capacities to grow. Embodying those values you never actually saw close up is something you can do for your children.

My hope in writing *Landscape of Mothers* is that the archetypes inspire a dialogue with yourself that brings awareness and understanding to where you are now with Motherhood, illuminates where you want to go, and offers direction for you to explore. May you find your whole and true Self amidst the demands, expectations, failures, and deep joys of Motherhood.

It is my intention that we can be parents who look back and say we did an okay job, with a slight smile of satisfaction on our faces. Perfect, no. But perfect is overrated and used for comparison, striving, and impressing other people. Landscape of Mothers is a process by which you find out what is really true about you, navigate your way through the messy and the difficult, and come out the other side feeling stronger and more connected to your beloveds (your Self, family, friends, community, village, etc.). You get to determine how, and if, and when, and what applies to you. You get to make up or write down or draw what is more true to you than what I present here. And I'll believe you. I already believe IN you.

I can only speak for myself, but I do this work because it makes my life better. Knowing myself—the influences from my past, my capacity to be with what is happening now, and my hopes for the future—allows me to see my own boundaries more clearly, to tap into my "yes" and my "no," to both cultivate my dreams and stay true to promises I've made. It helps me navigate my life in such a way that I can consciously tend to my children, my partner, my parents, my community, and myself in a way that doesn't leave anyone out, including myself.

Landscape of Mothers is a life map to helps us locate ourselves now—in our current struggles and joys. It also reveals some of the places we could go.

Even better, we get to our destination by choosing among multiple routes. Landscape of Mothers does not determine what our experiences will be along the way, which is up to us. It doesn't prescribe an answer, but offers up more possibilities. Working with Landscape of Mothers helps recognize our capacity for choice and alludes to the next step. The metaphor of map-as-life-path steps us back from our current experience, so we can see where we really want to go. Like a map, Landscape of Mothers provides us with a location, and it suggests how we move from one place to another. It's often easier to choose from a set of options rather than facing an open question.

This is not a "How To" sort of parenting book. Parenting advice changes and morphs over time depending on societal perspectives, cultural beliefs, family histories, and both the academic and personal understanding of child development. In fact, you aren't going to read much about children in this book, this is going to be about you. Because your children are going to learn from you. For better or worse, they'll take in everything about you. And, perhaps you've already noticed, they won't always interpret things like you think they will.

This book is a reclamation process for your own inner guidance system. If you were either neglected or micromanaged (or a million other versions of these things), you likely had damage done to the formation of your own inner adult. It is your inner guidance system that will help you be the parent you want to be. It is the way you will know what is correct for you as a parent.

Landscape of Mothers is about both making external changes and shifting internal perspective. Sometimes our greatest journey is to release our grip on certainty in order to see the beauty and possibility that lie before us. This allows spaciousness for curiosity and wonder.

Landscape of Mothers is a map built on three pillars or values. These pillars are sovereignty, regard, and relationship. Sovereignty is the ability to choose for ourselves. This gives us a sense of dignity that provides good ground for many of our other values. Regard is honor and respect. Anchored in our dignity, it is what allows us to feel worthy of being treated with kindness. It is also what we honor in others that reminds us that they too desire kindness. Relationship is connectedness, the recognition that we are in this together. What we choose affects others and vice versa.

These underlying principles to the Landscape of Mothers map may feel intangible, especially if they weren't part of the culture of your family of origin. So, if they sound like great words, but they seem far away, I understand. I want you to know that I am well aware that if you did not receive things like regard and dignity in your childhood, it's very difficult to know how to create a lived experience of them. It is not your fault or any failing of yours.

Archetypes can be helpful in the process of learning and exploring new ways of being. The Mothers can point us in the direction that we might learn from nature, and then we can set about the task of refining our relationship to those skills.

The Landscape of Mothers is organized to invite interaction with each archetype and exploration of each skill, so that they are present and accessible in our lived experience when we need them. That is, we practice in our day-to-day lives, so that we can access the core gifts of the Mothers when we need them most.

Our purpose here, with Landscape of Mothers archetypes, is to locate ourselves in the vast array of human-ness, and possibly to locate others with whom we are in relationship. This lets us better see the internal systems of care and expectations that drive our ability to be who we truly and wholly are becoming.

In this case, we can use the metaphor of ecology to take a look at ourselves. Nature has an inherent capacity to reflect our lives back to us. And so, looking to landscapes to reflect mothering is a natural fit.

Ultimately, this book is about connecting mothers back to nature with the intention of receiving guidance from the land around you and recalling the full range of yourself to bring to mothering. In short, figuring out how to live in ways that are conducive for life and love.

Let's meet the Landscape Mothers.

SUN AND MOON MOTHER

The poetry of the motion of celestial bodies lives in you.
~ Sun and Moon Mother

You find
Solid ground
In recalling you
~ Sun and Moon Mother

THE SUN AND MOON LANDSCAPE

The sun and moon are independent celestial bodies that are responsible for the rhythms of life on earth. They are each cyclical in their movements. What is true about either one in this moment may not be true later, but will be true again at some future time. Right now the sun is high in the sky. In four hours it will be approaching the horizon. Four hours after that it will be nowhere to be found. Twenty-four hours from now it will be right here again.

The sun is responsible for the seasons and oversees the growing cycle of many organisms on the earth. Thus, it is very much connected to our movement, our ability to get up and move through our days, and how we keep our own internal rhythms.

The moon is also going through cycles, ever waxing and waning. As it shifts and changes, so do the waters of the earth. Tidal patterns are created by the gravitational force of the moon. They are highest when the moon is dark or full because the moon's force is on the same axis as the sun's. Water is flexible and movable, and so it responds easily to the movements of the sun and moon. The moon's gravity affects all landscapes, but its influence is most easily observable in the tidal movement of the ocean. Our human bodies respond to these cycles and rhythms, keeping us in balance.

SUN AND MOON MOTHER

The Sun and Moon Mother is patterned on the luminaries that shine on earth. This luminosity represents our inner spark, the life force energy within us, the life that wants to be lived. As this light cycles, it needs to be tended. The strengths of Sun and Moon Mother are about taking care of this inner life, grounding it, protecting it, and cultivating space for listening to the wisdom of its voice.

Sun and Moon Mother is found in the cycle, the wheel of all things. She is more than the sum of her parts. She is the force that keeps things cohesive and interdependent, the gravitational force. She is the inherent drive toward connectedness, with others and also with ourselves. You experience her innate wisdoms as feelings of wholeness, harmony, balance, and resonance.

The cycles of the sun and moon reflect our own ability to step into our natural rhythms and cadence. Sun and Moon Mother helps us take these rhythms into our lives consciously, building on what helps us stay rooted and settled. We choose nourishing acts of daily care for ourselves and let go of those that leave us feeling rattled and scattered.

Sun and Moon Mother is the one who values our integration—our ability to wander through all of the Landscapes, cultivating our access to the strengths of each of the Mothers. She picks us up when we fall into the struggles of life and get stuck. She's the one who holds the spark of life force energy, who doesn't let us give up or fall into permanent despair.

Sun and Moon Mother is the integrator. She has the capacity to move us around the cycle, around the Landscapes, picking up important skills, awarenesses, and tools that we can use to meet any situation life presents to us. Her aim is to create healthy internal relationships with ourselves, to restore human relationship competency to our family, and to facilitate true belonging with a group or community.

The resourced and regulated Sun and Moon Mother is the internal voice that lets us know when it's time to let go, or that it's time to get up and do what needs to be done. She sets us straight and reminds us of what we really know is true. Sometimes it's easy to settle into a pattern, one perspective, one place in the Landscape. Sun and Moon Mother reminds us that while rest time is appropriate, we cannot stay in just one aspect of ourselves for too long. We risk becoming fragmented or partitioned. We lose access to other parts of our inner psychic landscape.

STRENGTHS OF SUN AND MOON MOTHER

To more deeply explore the strengths of Sun and Moon Mother, it's useful to consider the sun and the moon separately. We know the sun of this Mother as the warmth—the active, the doing, and the activation part of our regulation. That is, what we do directly impacts how we feel. In a body-centered way, we could see the sun as the sympathetic nervous system, which is the part that prepares us to be active, focused, and attentive. It is also the part of our nervous system that reacts to stress with fighting, defiance, resistance, or fleeing. Recall that we're not judging the reaction as "bad." They are stress responses that have their place.

And we can perceive the moon of this Mother to be the soft, the dark, the reflective, the resting part of our regulation. In the body-centered approach, she is the parasympathetic nervous system, which is focused on resting, digesting food, and repairing tissues. This part of the nervous system reacts to stress with trying to calm everyone down, getting quiet, acquiescing, or shutting down. Again, none of these are bad or wrong.

The primary strength of Sun and Moon Mother then, is regulation between these two systems. The sun tends to drive action and the moon brings forward rest and repair. The ability to have access to both is what allows us to increase our capacity to be with others in healthy relationship. Knowing how and when to tap into action or calm is the basis for being present in parenting. When we create practices and rhythms in our lives that support this flow back and forth, we are cultivating one of the tools missing from the parenting books: regulation. We learn to self-soothe and self-regulate so that we can offer this same skill to our children. Sun and Moon Mother is our best ally for flowing between presence and our own renewal.

How we move through these cycles of activation and rest is our life rhythm. It is the way our lives feel steady amidst the constant movement and change. It is how we anchor ourselves in our every day, and it determines how well we are able to be true to ourselves and our family members. This is the seed of everything that we want to grow, and it is the center to which we can always return when challenges arise.

Activation time and rest time each provide us with a sense of renewal. Rest restores energy and ability to think clearly, while activation and motion is often inspiring and creates curiosity and playfulness. This is the nourishment of our every day—balance between activity and rest, external world and internal world.

Sun and Moon Mother is made up of the small things, the movements and moments that can seem insignificant in and of themselves, but that keep the world moving and life force energy flowing. She nudges us to take small, incremental steps and to keep going. She encourages us to move through iteration; that is, to do one small thing, then build one more small thing on the first one, and then one more after that. Every so often, check back in to make sure the direction you're headed is still the one you want.

STRUGGLES OF SUN AND MOON MOTHER

When Sun and Moon Mother isn't able to weave her cycles into wholeness, she becomes fragmented. Her energy is scattered and leaks out everywhere without creating anything of value for her. She is left exhausted and wrung out.

This kind of exhaustion, and the inability to tap back into her life force energy are so depleting that she runs the risk of getting stuck in one of the Landscapes. Once stuck, it's hard to remember what we know about getting ourselves going again. She forgets what she knows, and is probably too tired to make it happen anyway. If this becomes her home Landscape she will collapse. She will give up. Her nervous system will be so overwhelmed that she will find it impossible to move.

Coherence is a sense of being "in line" with yourself. Things that pit head and heart and gut against each other get in the way of coherence. In other words, disrupters of coherence make you feel torn between what your heart believes and what your gut says. Disrupters are made of whatever beliefs set your needs against the needs of others, or cause you to be the one who gets shorted.

Feeling like you're bushwhacking your way through life rather than walking your path is one way you know that you're in the struggles of Sun and Moon Mother. That isn't to say things will always be easy, but they don't have to be extra hard either. You don't get gold stars for struggling.

Common pitfalls for Sun and Moon Mother are beliefs like: "if I'm working hard I'm doing it well," or "if I work harder I am more lovable," or "if I work extra hard it must mean I really care about it / him / her / them." These are signs that we've been taught to give up our energy or sense of self in order to serve someone else. These thoughts aren't true, and they are usually at odds with the strengths of Sun and Moon Mother which revolve around self-regulation. If you feel like you're struggling with the rules of "how things are," or "it's just how the world works," it's likely you learned these rules before you were able to think about whether or not you agreed. It's also helpful to know that they are unspoken rules in some family and cultural dynamics. But they don't have to be in your family going forward. It's possible to orient toward being inherently lovable, not having to prove your worth, and a dynamic where caring is about tending rather than sacrifice.

Sun and Moon Mother holds the skills that help us get back on our path—not just any path, and not the path someone else designed for us or wishes we would take, but our very own path of all that is rightly ours. This is a very common pitfall: to end up on a journey that is not of our own making, but which was handed to us before we ever really understood what we wanted our lives to be about.

Sun and Moon Mother thrives on embodiment. She advocates for following our innate rhythms and the cycles of nature, and for rooting into the things that nourish and protect us. The lack of motion—the stagnancy—threatens her very life. She has to begin to move around the Landscape and tap into other parts of herself. She needs to root back into her wholeness.

SUN AND MOON MOTHER IN PARENTING

Since Sun and Moon Mother is deeply rooted in cycling and process, she really represents the contrast between being willing to let things stay as they currently are and the desire for things to be different. That is, parenting is a pivotal commitment moment. Will you parent as you were parented? Or do you want your parenting to be different? Who do you want to be as a parent?

If your parents held the same awarenesses and values when you were a child that you currently hold, then you are likely to be happy with your childhood experience. You may choose to repeat what your parents did. You place importance on the stability of experience: on the fact that you still hold the same values you grew up with, and that what was true for you will be true for your children.

My guess is that you're reading this book because you have something different in mind (whatever that is, even if you can't articulate it yet). You're not interested in working off your parents' playbook. Your values and awareness are different than your parents. However, you don't have a map because what happened to you either doesn't apply anymore, or wasn't something you want repeated.

You might also be engaged with Landscape of Mothers because you're looking to build the capacity of the Adult in you who needs to care for your Inner Child. You might identify more with wanting to create security and internal kindness, and find a new way to care for yourself that nourishes you instead of judging you as not enough.

Either way, Sun and Moon Mother is the one stoking your discontent. She is telling you there is a way, but that it's your own, and it'll be up to you to make decisions about how to move around. She's nudging you to visit the Landscapes and to build a relationship with the wisdom in each.

THE INNATE GIFT OF SUN AND MOON MOTHER

Renewal is Sun and Moon Mother's innate gift. She stands for opting out of the disconnection of our busy and isolated lives, and into reclamation, soul nourishment, and deep connection. She stands for autonomy and the full expression of your uniqueness as well as a deep sense of true belonging. It's not as much about "having it all" as it is about making sure that all parts of you get nourished.

The way to Sun and Moon Mother's wisdom is through spaciousness and regulating our pace. We are often so busy, so focused on our own lives and the immediate To Do list, that there isn't enough time, quiet, and slowness to hear our own heart. When we are busy it is harder to know what we need, and sometimes it's even harder to ask for it.

Renewal most often happens in a million tiny moments, through doing small things that have a big impact. These things are easy to overlook, especially if we are engaged in the constant motion of our fast-paced world. The practice of checking in with our senses is the glue of our lives, when we orient toward what feels good and right, and create space and time to settle and hear our hearts.

The practices of Sun and Moon Mother are whatever brings us a sense of feeling rooted, secure, and attentive. They are the things that help us return to our center, that renew our sense of being and fullness. Renewal is a spring, a consistent source of something needed, a deep well of continued nurturance. It is the practice of arising, of emananting or evolving from a source. And so the invitation of Sun and Moon Mother is to join the rhythms of nature, even if just for a moment, to listen, and to allow awareness of the next right thing to arise.

A wise Grandmother once told me that the healing we seek comes from understanding what is missing and bringing it to the situation. Our healing can be facilitated by, but does not complete itself through, the telling of the story, or the commitment to the details. It comes in the fulfillment of unmet needs. The first step is to know the unmet need by feeling and acknowledging it. The second step is to develop a series of small actions that fulfill the need and facilitate a sense of safety and structure for nervous system regulation.

CULTIVATING SUN AND MOON MOTHER

Somatic practices can help us integrate our thoughtful awareness into our actions. Through our bodies we can process and understand our thoughts in a different way. The following activities are suggestions for how you might begin to interact with Sun and Moon Mother through your body in addition to reading about her.

Sun and Moon Mother Question: What needs renewing and restoring?

Sun and Moon Mother Activity

The first step in renewal is usually to step back from whatever has been pushing on you. We get off balance when we're pushed off our center and lose our nourishing rhythms. We start to falter, to feel uncertain, to waver. Therefore, the first order of business is to step back from whatever feels like it's pushing on you, at least temporarily.

Most often what is pushing us is our own mind. It is telling us how things should be instead of working with what is. Our thoughts may frequently go to the future—so our tasks begin to feel urgent and we feel "behind" (and we are, because we're trying to live tomorrow, but it's right now). Tension accrues.

So the invitation for renewal is to simply stop, put your hand on your heart or your belly. If you feel like you're spinning, sit down and firmly press your hands into your thighs. Take a slow, full breath, in through your nose and out through your mouth. Repeat. This stops the forward motion of the pushing and the spinning mind, and allows you to recenter right here, right now.

Going Deeper with Sun and Moon Mother

Lasting change happens incrementally and by iteration. Small steps taken over and over help you move toward yourself in a sustainable way. You do not have to take big leaps of faith.

The number one request of Sun and Moon Mother is for you to settle into your own rhythms and structures. To do this, it is helpful to start noticing the little things. What do you do each morning? Consciously or unconsciously, how do the things you do set you on a path through your day, week, season, year?

Our days are cycles, and when we mark these repetitions with attention and intention, we punctuate them with meaning. So where can we hook into these cycles? Where can we find the thread of our lives and create intention to touch back in with that thread regularly? What do we carry as a habit or necessity that is already marking our days? How can we make it more intentional, more fulfilling, and anchoring?

Begin a notebook, or sticky notes, or however you can keep track of some of these regulating habits. Write down three things you currently and regularly do in the morning when you get up. Common things we do every morning: check the phone, make coffee, and get in the shower. The list could also include: feeding pets, checking messages, and reading the news. Notice where these seemingly small activities take your attention. Does it feel good when that's where your attention goes in the morning? If not, what else would you like to try instead?

Regulation is about having a small set of actions, preferably beginning with things you already do, that make you feel settled into your life. When you ritualize those things—that is, when you touch into their meaning for you while you do them—they can become moments of grace in your day that feed you rather than deplete you. These can be small things you do anytime during the day, but that you do each day at approximately the same time.

WIND MOTHER

The breeze is an invitation to dance with your own breath.

~ Wind Mother

What is

Singing in

The depths of your breath

~ Wind Mother

THE WIND LANDSCAPE

If you're thinking that wind might be more elemental and less of a land-scape, you're right. However, Wind Mother was actually one of the first that came when this project found me. In fact, I've said more than once that she's the one who wrote this book. She is the initiator, and therefore I see her as a part of the Landscape.

The wind is full of motion, and that motion has different qualities. Sometimes it moves quickly, sometimes gently. Trees topple in its wake, and it stirs up the surface of oceans. The wind moves water and dust around the planet, picking things up and dropping them again. It dis-perses seeds, moving life around to new areas, helping new life to find good ground in which to begin again.

The wind in the body is the breath, and so it corresponds to the flow of breathing and speaking. Wind Mother is associated with our mental capacities... particularly the way we put words to thoughts. Maybe that's because of the motion of our thoughts, the sense that thinking a bunch can lift us up off the ground—as in flights of fancy, or going nowhere, just spinning our wheels. Either way, the sense is that too much airiness gets us off the ground, for better or worse.

Wind is also the movement of mixing, shifting, and reorganizing. The air is rarely truly still. It is the breath of the Earth, the inhale and the exhale that keeps the life force energy circulating. Without wind things become stagnant and heavy.

WIND MOTHER

Wind Mother flows and circulates, carrying thought and possibility on her breath. She sows seeds by distributing them across the landscape, drawing attention outward and onward. The Wind Mother draws your dreams out of you and spreads them out, encouraging you to follow them.

She encourages thinking outside the box and trying something new. She is a lover of ideas, and a believer in the magic of what can happen if we follow our gut instincts. She ignites inspiration to live by your own values, rather than the dogma at hand. Wind Mother wants sovereign truth to be expressed and voiced. She wants you to do what you came here to do. And she knows that sometimes it's easy to choose to stay in one place because it feels stable. You know Wind Mother is active in your life when she pushes you out of your cozy nest!

Wind Mother is about being uprooted and unhooked from what we know. She is about picking things up and carrying them to another place. This is often where we lose the anchors of our "regular" ways of being. It is where our habits and reactions lead us to unexpected and often uncomfortable places.

She is the spark inside of you that will keep you going when you feel like you're all out of juice. Wind Mother is especially persistent about the things that nourish you and fill you up. She is the one who pulls you toward your desires, keeping you going even when you think you want to give up.

Wind Mother can go too far, pushing for change without checking to see if everything is ready. She often needs boundaries (pushing right up against her neighbor, Desert Mother). Wind Mother will go anywhere, into the cracks and crevices, through the open windows, and across the prairies. She'll push the envelope every chance she gets.

STRENGTHS OF WIND MOTHER

Wind Mother, as you might imagine, changes easily and is quite flexible. She doesn't linger too long in one place, preferring instead the adventure and momentum of movement. Wind Mother brings inspiration and possibility your way. When she blows through your life, she asks you to keep moving, keep taking steps toward your dreams.

Having a first baby (really any baby, or taking a leap with any big project or commitment) is one such moment. One in which you decide you're ready to be a parent, or at least willing to try. Wind Mother has been in you, opening up possibility, a new path, maybe a completely different direction than you had been going. She's nudging you out of your comfort zone, out of your routine, and into a whole new world.

Wind Mother is good at beginnings. Whether it's a true beginning, like a new start on an old project, or just an adjustment to an ongoing process, the Wind Mother beckons you to change your path. She's good at inquiry, curiosity, and hope. She supports and lifts the heart in the direction of its dreams.

Wind Mother is usually gentle, quiet, kind, and reassuring. She believes in teaching by example. She knows that demands rarely get us what we need or want in relationships. She is a pragmatist and generally opts instead for kind, compassionate conversation. She encourages her children as they explore, expand, and try on new ways of being.

She has the gifts of insight and intuition. Intuitive knowing requires trusting one's internal sensations, understanding the meaning of what we feel, and being able to translate that into some kind of action.

Wind Mother also contains wonder. The ability to be inspired by the mundane, to see beauty in the stuff of everyday, and to be awed by the insignificant. She invites curiosity and attentiveness.

Wonder is made of the ability to see the sacred in the common and usual. We engage with wonder when we can hold on to the mystery and magical inspiration of discovery. We flirt with it when we nurture the beauty in ourselves and others for what it actually is. Wonder gives us the touch of kindness, not just for each other, but for all living beings, and for the Earth that is our home. We begin to see and feel the presence of the wild places, not only in our outer world, but also in our inner landscape.

When we feel certain, it undermines our sense of wonder—and it works against Wind Mother. Without wonder, without the embrace of uncertainty, there is a great risk of choosing to keep things the same instead of stepping into new perspectives, instead of finding the spaciousness that lets us shift into meaning and connection.

STRUGGLES OF WIND MOTHER

One of the difficulties of Wind Mother is that she can be ungrounded. She might move so much that she seems to have no roots at all, or she may avoid the uncomfortable things in life that really do need tending. Wind Mother can be unpredictable, which is a trait in a caregiver that can be difficult for a child.

Wind Mother can also be timid and ambivalent. That is, she finds it difficult to stand for things, even if she values them greatly. Her ability to see the complexity and feel the needs of everyone around her make it hard to choose a side and take a stand. She is a people-pleaser. This is partly because her intuitive senses are so strong and she knows what's needed by a group, as well as what individuals are feeling. When she defaults to trying to please everyone, she loses her strength around what's important to her.

Her ambivalence, or inability to stand strongly, may lead her to avoid going deep. Her strong intuition leads her to see the big picture, the complexity, and it can feel overwhelming. Besides, she's okay with change, so maybe it's just easier if she moves on rather than trying to figure out how to meet and navigate the difficulty.

Wind Mother can be avoidant of depth of feeling as well as depth of relationship. She might prefer to keep things light and happy, avoiding the parts of life that feel hard and unpleasant. This can keep her from truly seeing others for who they are and what they need. She can give off the vibe that she's not interested in things that don't make her happy, so it's hard to go to her for help when you have a problem. She tends to dismiss difficulty and bypass painful truths.

WIND MOTHER IN PARENTING

Wind Mother knows that women are the vessels through which their children arrive on the planet. Women are the beginning, the tenders of this life. There is no guarantee of who this being who comes into the world is going to become—a mother's job is simply to teach and guide as best she can. The child is its own being, and arrives with some patterning already in place. Every mother with more than one child knows that they arrive with their own personalities. Every baby is so different.

The unknown lives inside Wind Mother—a sowing of seeds that is unpredictable in its nature and potential. She is the Mother who knows how little she controls. Wind Mother knows that her children will grow and leave home. They are gathering the tools they need for moving on. She prepares them as seeds that will ride her winds to new grounds, where they will sprout and grow new roots and possibly nurture the next generation.

While every mother envisions her child growing into an adult and maybe even having their own kids, Wind Mother knows there is unpredictability in the world. All we can really do is cultivate trust and resilience. We are all destined to walk with Wind Mother.

In some ways, Wind Mother could also be known as the Mother Who Reinvents Herself. As kids grow and change and life unfolds, they need different things from their mothers. The flexibility of Wind Mother allows her to sway with her children, learning as they go, shifting and changing her ways as needed. Sometimes women say they "grew up" with their children, and in the best ways I think they're referring to how mothering kept them learning and adapting in their relationships with their children. This knowledge and understanding can be applied to other relationships in life that are strained. Perhaps they need a little Wind Mother energy.

A depleted Wind Mother is one who avoids and has difficulty listening and seeing others. She keeps moving in order not to feel too deeply, and wants to appear happy and resists anything that threatens that veneer. She is a mother that children don't trust. She can't sit still long enough to be predictable, she doesn't have the groundedness to feel trustworthy, and her children won't be likely to go to her when they need help.

THE INNATE GIFT OF WIND MOTHER

Wind Mother's unshakable gift is trust. Trust, in our daily life, is made of listening—both listening to one another and to ourselves.

Trust. This might be the one I avoided the longest. Trust isn't easy for a person who learned that peers were more likely to torment you than play with you, and adults were useless as advocates for justice or even simple integrity. But it turns out it's a life skill, whether I want it to be or not.

We can get away with being skeptical and arms-length-ish with other adults. But kids don't really let that happen. It turns out that raising children elevates trust to an art form.

Learning to trust begins with trying it out on ourselves. As new parents, we have to figure out communication with this new baby, and there's no choice but to keep trying when we're uncertain. We have to trust in ourselves to "get it," and we have to trust them to help us get there. The first years are mostly nonverbal attempts at connection, relationship, and working out needs.

Trust in ourselves gives us the flexibility to navigate uncertain times.

And then, as our children grow, we have to continue to trust them. There are definitely times where we just have to let them figure out things on their own. We have to believe that they will come to us when they need guidance.

Trust allows us to come together when difficulties arise.

Eventually, we even have to trust that if something difficult happens that we'll handle it together—that no one will be left alone to figure it out in isolation. Or, if they do have to go forward and handle it alone, that they'll have the resources and skills to do that.

Trust gives us the ability to let go when they go into the world on their own.

All along, while we're stretching our trust in our children to remarkable capacity, we are also stretching our trust in ourselves further than we imagined possible. We have to believe that we have been good enough parents. We have to have confidence that if the very worst that our mind conjures come to pass, that we will have the resources and support to get through it.

Trust allows us to believe in our own resilience and strength, too.

I have learned over the years that trust is built via our relationships. The quality of how we interact in small, everyday moments turns out to be the foundation for an orientation of trust. It rests on a belief in the capacity of the family to be there for each other and to have each other's best interests at heart. Trust is as ungraspable as the wind... and yet the impacts of both are significant and widespread.

CULTIVATING WIND MOTHER

Body centered practice integrates our mind's awareness into our actions. We get a chance to think differently or see from a new perspective. The following activities are suggestions for how you might begin to interact with Wind Mother through noticing her wisdom in your body.

The Wind Mother Question: What needs to be released?

Wind Mother Activity

Breathing is a cycle that supports the life in our cells. Our breath connects us with other living beings as oxygen and carbon dioxide move in and out of our bodies. This is our connection with Spirit or Life Force Energy. This is where we can place our trust—in the movement patterns that, without our conscious knowledge or direction, keep life force energy flowing.

Find a quiet moment and place. Feel yourself resting on the earth. Invite relaxation into any muscle you're not actively using to hold your posture right now. Notice how as you relax further, you continue to be held by the earth under you. Feel the solidity of that support. Allowing your body to rest into the support of the ground under you. Notice your breath.
As your body finds the relaxation available in this moment, notice if/how your breath changes. Often there is an opening of the chest and torso, such that the breath comes a little easier.

Notice how your breath is one of your primary life support processes. Consider how your breath supports you and your body. Do you feel more alive when you place some attention on your breath, as we did in this exercise? Do you tend to hold your breath or limit it in some way?

Going Deeper with Wind Mother

Get comfortable for a short meditation. It's akin to a body scan which is sometimes done in somatic work.

Close your eyes and allow your body to settle into position. Feel the floor beneath you and the breath in your body. This is the earth element and the air element deeply present in how you already are. No extra work.

Begin at the top of the head, slowly making your way down your body to your toes. At each place you stop, breathe into that space (that is, simply breathe with your attention focused at that particular location).

Noticing your head, your mind, your sensory organs. Breathe in and out, keeping your awareness at your head. Bring your presence to this particular part of your body.

Move your attention down to your neck and shoulders. With each inhale, intend that area to receive what it needs to feel safe, cared for, and appreciated. With each exhale, invite a release of any tension that might be there.
Move attention to your chest, heart, and lungs. Tension can be in the chemistry, in the tissues, or in the muscles. We tend to only notice muscle tension, so if you don't feel your muscles release, that's okay.

Bring your attention to your arms, hands, and fingers. The release could be a mental perspective that doesn't apply to you, or it could be something you were taught about how the world works that you no longer agree with. It could also be literal muscle tension.

Notice your belly, lower back, and hips. Try not to judge, but to go for the feeling that things in you are working together in a way they hadn't before.

Now, bring attention to your legs, knees, calves, and feet. Again, you don't have to be able to write a report on it. If you feel it, that's enough. If you don't feel it, trust that your body is doing what it can, and it isn't forcing itself to do things it can't.

Lastly, allow your awareness to diffuse through your whole body. Notice that the parts we chose were not separate. They depend on one another. Breathe into that whole-being awareness with the intent to deliver what is needed. Then breathe out, release tension, and notice how all of the parts can weave with the others to create the whole.

Note: I'll be the first to admit that cultivating trust is inherently a tricky business. We can't force it or decide it. Trust comes from within. It comes from building on the small steps of cycle and rhythm that we began with Sun and Moon Mother. We use the things we already know and trust about how our nervous systems respond to our rhythms, and we intentionally lean into those. That's where we start. In this meditation, we begin with the breath. We know how to do that.

Trust takes time to build. Wounds have to be tended. Often, we need someone else's help with that, because we don't heal social wounds and sense-of-self wounds in isolation. Wind Mother asks us to cultivate enough trust to take a chance on healing. To listen to the voices in the world and feel the truth emanating from some of them is to begin to put words to the inner experiences that we could never name before.

When we take a small step toward trusting ourselves, we normalize our experiences and our feelings. From there we learn to trust that we will also find other people who feel deeply like we do. We will find others who are healing the wounds as we are. It takes some vulnerability—not the oversharing kind, but the willingness kind. The willingness to listen to others, feel our shared experiences in our bodies, and learn to stand gently and firmly for what we value.

This is reflected in the end of the meditation, where we notice that the body parts are truly interconnected. We can extend this to our internal "parts" (i.e. the one in us who is scared, the one in us that had a particular experience, the one in us that felt alone). We can also extend the idea that, just as our body parts are connected and interdependent, so are the parts of our psyche. By beginning with the body, we can orient to the idea that we already have one particular kind of experience of being in it together (a physical one), and we can extend that experience to our mental or emotional parts as well. No part in us is alone.

We can begin by trusting Wind Mother herself. The seeds she spreads are small. Some of them won't come to much, but she's instrumental to the ones that will. She's all the small, seemingly inconsequential moments that combine into something that, when we look back, was full of grace, happenstance, and deep trust. She is the one in us that won't settle, the one that continually invites us toward what we want and need.

Wind Mother is about the things that are so easy to overlook... joy, freedom, gratitude, exploration, curiosity. We focus on the struggles, but in many ways, my experience of the Wind Mother is that she tries to lift us out of the doldrums, pulling us upward and forward, reminding us of the luminosity (from Sun and Moon Mother) that is drawing us in the direction of our meaningful life.

DESERT MOTHER

The details in the desert are small and fleeting. And they are equally astounding to any other place you might know. Look close enough to discern the wondrous from the mundane. ~ Desert Mother

Perceive

Boundaries

As your self respect

~ Desert Mother

THE DESERT LANDSCAPE

The desert is wide-open country for the most part. It is expansive, vast, exposed, and dry. There is spaciousness in the desert. There are big skies, and long impressive horizons. It can also be the place of exposure and sun-bleached bones. Death and stillness are obvious parts of life in the desert.

Water and nourishment are scarce in the desert environment… hence the stillness. Most living things are waiting for the waters to soften them so that they can bloom, move, reproduce, or eat. The smallest amounts of nourishment create full expressions. When water is detected, life goes for it, giving all it has before settling back down to wait for the next downpour.

Desert resources are unpredictable and rare. There is no abundance laying around unused. It is efficient and everything is utilized. Recycling happens quickly and nothing is left behind.

It's also a place where clear decisions are made, where behavior is determined by life and death. If life is the answer, then the question becomes how to take care of oneself at the most basic but critical levels. "What do I need?" is a constant refrain.

DESERT MOTHER

At her best, Desert Mother is resourceful and places high value on autonomy and individuality. She is independent, self-focused, and opportunistic. She lives in the moment and is ready to respond when conditions become favorable.

Desert Mother brings spaciousness to everything. She responds with care, waiting for the right time and place and way. Sometimes what she brings is stillness, because she knows that in the waiting our own truths and understandings can arise. It is sometimes true that time heals a wound.

This waiting can take many forms. Desert creatures often seek shade and respite from the relentless daytime sun. That can take the form of sleeping during the day and being awake at night, or it can mean finding spaces in cracks or crevices, or underground.

Desert Mother builds on the trust of Wind Mother to believe in the natural development of her children. She knows that each child is different, with different needs, and she is willing to see what emerges and unfolds before taking action. She knows she doesn't have to figure out what comes next, but she does need to tend to it when it arises.

She is patient, generous with space, and sparse on direction. Her inputs come in the form of questions—inviting others to search themselves for an answer, rather than putting forth her own solution. She tends toward guidance over advice.

Desert Mother doesn't do excess. What she offers is simple, neat, and elegant. No unnecessary movements or adornments. After all, the bottom line in the desert is that resources are scarce. There is no such thing as long-term abundance, so nothing will be wasted.

STRENGTHS OF DESERT MOTHER

When well-resourced, Desert Mother tends to be confident in herself and her children. She trusts that both their successes and failures continue to develop them as human beings. She knows that overcoming adversity is important for building confidence and resourcefulness. Curiosity and guidance are part of that development, and she's available for that too. It's like when the rains come and everything soaks up the water and blooms. Desert Mother knows when to slow down, soak in the waters, create space, and look for the next right step.

Desert Mother is a master of guidance rather than advice. In our world, which values speed and efficiency, it often feels easier to tell someone what we think they should do, rather than use our curiosity to provide a path for others to find their own way. Desert Mother understands that what we discover for ourselves is much more powerful and enduring than what is given as directions.

Wind Mother provides the trust, but Desert Mother takes this to everyday life. She utilizes her trust in natural processes, and in the way she knows things to be, and she allows those processes to hold her as she moves through parenting. In her best moments, she is adaptable and aware of what is needed. Desert Mother provides knowing guidance for her child, producing a sense of self in the child—a conviction that their inner world and inner knowing are valid and trustworthy. This child can grow up to be self-sufficient, self-aware, and confident.

The strength of Desert Mother lies in her ability to reflect, honor, and support healthy boundaries in her children. Rather than rules and regulations, she offers curiosity and thoughtfulness. This provides a sense of autonomy in her children. They have their own center and edges. They are self-defined, and respected in that self-definition.

Desert Mother is good at boundaries. She knows how to say "no" in a way that is comfortable for her. She knows how to say "yes" only to the things she really wants or feels are important. With increasing capability, she is also able to say "no" to something she deems important but knows that she lacks the resources to do.

Because she is clear about providing only what is truly needed, she tends not to overdo it, and has free time on her hands. Her opportunity, should she choose it, would be to do her own personal work. Good personal boundaries help Desert Mother understand that her child is their own person. She knows that the child's emotions and struggles are not her own. In fact, a healthy Desert Mother understands this in all of her relationships.

I will venture to guess that someone who naturally expresses the strengths of Desert Mother had parents who respected their boundaries and autonomy. For those of us who experienced boundary violations as children, or had caregivers that had wounds in the landscape of Desert Mother, this is probably an area of deep work. You are not alone and there is nothing wrong with you. Your awareness and dedication to boundaries and clarity in relationships will make this journey significantly easier. Desert Mother is set up nicely for this.

STRUGGLES OF DESERT MOTHER

Desert Mother's apparent strength of trusting inner guidance can actually be a pitfall if her inner guidance system has been damaged. If she endured abuse or suffering that resulted in a corruption of her own system of knowing herself, she may not be good at discerning what is true, needed, or valuable. She may be driven by her wounds and unable to tell the difference between external forces and her internal wisdom.

Desert Mother struggles with violated boundaries. If lack of boundaries and responsibility was or is a characteristic of her origin family, she can either become enmeshed in her family relationships or avoid them. Either way, it is hard for her to allow her desires to inform her direction. When I say "desires," I'm not talking about her whims, but the emergence of her inner knowing and wisdom.

This difficulty with accessing her own center can leave her prone to not being able to recognize or respect the autonomy of others. If the boundaries she overrides are not only her own, but those of her children, it becomes easy to perpetuate the wounds. Desert Mother may not mean to repeat harmful behaviors, but it is difficult to change family patterns if she continues to have poor boundaries.

This lack of boundaries can also leave us, as mothers, open to allowing our children to violate our boundaries. That is, they can behave in ways that are unacceptable to us, but we do not have the skills to stand for our own boundaries with kindness. Alternatively, we may have learned so deeply that our needs don't matter that we choose to violate our own boundaries by always putting others first or never taking good enough care of ourselves.

Desert Mother struggles with knowing how and when to enforce or reflect boundaries, leaving children to figure things out on their own. She may not be good at nuanced or flexible boundaries, which are essential requirements of mothering. Children need to be held differently as they grow and mature. They need different reflections and guidance. This evolution can be difficult for Desert Mother who did not have these experiences as a child.

DESERT MOTHER IN PARENTING

Desert Mother knows that her child enters this world already a unique individual. Babies have innate characteristics and are born with their own disposition. Thus, Desert Mother orients herself in parenting to managing the child minimally, making space for their personal preferences and quirks. She values space for her child to build their own framework for how to be in the world. She supports their self-awareness and their internal assessment of their needs and desires. Desert Mother would rather have a self-directed child than a compliant one.

She believes in the strength and resilience of people, including her children. She raises clever and independent children who know their own minds and have confidence in their ability to solve problems and create whatever they set their sights on.

The struggles of Desert Mother might be seen in someone who is actively managing her childhood wounds. She may be feeling the pains come up as her children reach the ages of her own wounds, or the pains may come up through circumstance. Either way she's juggling raising children and tending to her personal growth at the same time. She may begin this journey by trying to relegate memories to the past, but as her children continue to grow she finds that these issues regularly pop up.

A woman who is raising children while simultaneously addressing her own wounds can be stretched thin emotionally. She may find all she has left for mothering is the moments or energy in between her personal healing, when she is somewhat free to tend, nurture, and nourish her offspring. This is a tricky place, because as a culture, we tend to blame these women for their lack of nourishment for themselves and their kids. We blame them for the inability to, alone, meet every need of their children. This is one of the places that mothers can feel stuck. They cannot live up to expectations, and they get blamed for "coming up short" on an impossible task.

When Desert Mother is struggling and needs help, she tends to not be good at finding, asking for, or letting people know that she needs assistance. In a culture that glorifies the idea that we can all do everything for ourselves, Desert Mother may find it hard to even admit she deserves help and is often loath to admit that she needs it.

She is a minimalist at heart, but the danger is in not being enough. While Desert Mother doesn't hover over her child, she is watching and notices when it is time to give guidance. Her advice will be rare, and in the best circumstances it instills a sense of self-confidence in her children. However, the risk is that the child needs more than she realizes, and so the child feels abandoned or undernourished.

THE INNATE GIFT OF DESERT MOTHER

The core gift of Desert Mother is boundaries. That is, she feels them, whether she has had positive reinforcing experiences or negative ones that decimated her boundaries. She is innately aware that something is needed—some separation that allows a sense of self to develop, so the self can relate honestly and openly with others.

For Desert Mother, boundaries are not as simple as being able to say "yes" or "no." That is important for basic boundaries, true. But, Desert Mother has a richer vision of boundaries. When you are a caregiver, it can be necessary to prioritize others' needs over your own. It comes with the territory. So, for a woman with unclear boundaries before children, it's easy for them to get further undermined when she becomes a caregiver.

Desert Mother considers boundaries with others (how others can treat you), internal boundaries (how you treat yourself), and boundaries that others place (how others let you treat them). These all inform one another.

When we think of boundaries we usually envision them in the context of ourselves and someone else. This is where knowing our "yes" and our "no" comes in handy. We make agreements with others about how they are allowed to treat us based on these boundaries.

Boundaries that you hold for yourself encompass both how you talk to yourself and how you decide what's necessary to do. Part of this is taking a look at how your inner voice works and what you allow it to say about and to you. This inner voice often reflects the dynamics of your family of origin and will continue to operate by those rules, even as you grow and make different agreements. A lot of people have inner voices that are far more critical, rude, and cruel than anything they would let anyone else say to them out loud.

We also set interior boundaries around things we have to do because they need to be done, like brushing teeth and doing the dishes. We tend to not like them, but we have rules that we adhere to because they simply need to be done for health and well-being.

Boundaries others set with us are about how others allow us to treat them. They are entwined with how we perceive others want to be treated, and how we want to treat them. Sometimes these are tough and can feel like rejection or dismissal. Desert Mother is good at this though, as she is willing and able to see other people as independent and autonomous, doing what they need to be doing.

Boundaries often need to be flexible because they are not applicable to every situation or person. Certain times may call for something unexpected. Desert Mother does this with grace and clarity. She is able to name what is true, because she trusts her own feelings and knowing.

Difficulties with boundaries might come up as we move away from the old perspective of bad and good, right and wrong. When we determine for ourselves what our right actions are, we will inevitably conflict with what others expect of us. We will have to stand for our choices. Desert Mother tends to opt for valuing her uniqueness and individuality over conformity. Because we all want to belong, as well as to be accepted as ourselves, this can lead to loneliness.

Another strain on boundaries is the perceived need to please others in order to create a sense of personal safety. If your sense of safety depends on the moods and regulation of others, I recommend looking to Sun and Moon Mother for a refresher in self-regulation.

Know that discernment is needed when creating healthy boundaries. There is a difference between needing boundaries and taking care of your bottom line for basic safety. Discernment is the granularity of knowing if and when to apply boundaries, how, and with whom.

CULTIVATING DESERT MOTHER

Somatic practices help us connect our new awareness and our actions. We practice new thoughts and behaviors by moving them through our bodies and creating a lived experience. The following activities are suggestions for how you might get to know Desert Mother through your body experience.

The Desert Mother Question: What needs to be protected?

Desert Mother Activity

Sit down somewhere you won't be interrupted for at least 5 minutes. Take a breath, focusing your attention on your body. Notice how your body presses down on Earth (gravity) and how Earth meets your feet and holds you up. Notice your skin as the physical boundary of your body. Feel your clothes, notice the way the air moves, and make note of the temperature on your skin.

Now notice that there is a space around your body. There is a sphere at arms length out from your body—all the way around—above you, below you, to your left, and your right, in front of you, and behind. Notice how big that "sphere" is. This is the proprioceptive space, or the space that the brain is aware that you could move into at any moment. It's the space that you take up if you include the ways you could move your arms or legs from where you are now. The brain maps all of this space for you without thinking about it. It's the reason you can sit at a desk and take your hand from your lap to the desktop without hitting the table. Your brain knows where the table is and where your hand is without looking at them.

This is your boundary in the most general sense. It already exists. It is not something you need to create. The more you notice and sit with it, the more it will take on definition. It will feel more "real." I encourage you to reach your arms out and "draw" this sphere in the air around you to the best of your ability. Really reach out, and imagine that your fingertips are drawing this boundary in the air.

You can either stop here, or go on with the next exercise. If you stop here, stop moving your arms and settle into your core. Notice the boundary from where you sit. Feel it. Your brain has already mapped this space around you, and this exercise is reinforcing the fact that you occupy a space in the world, and that you have definition.

Going Deeper with Desert Mother

If you took a break and are now sitting down to go deeper, begin again with the Boundaries Activity then continue here. You'll also need to add at least 5 minutes to your timer.

Physical boundaries are determined by our skin, and our brain-mapped boundaries are at approximately arms length all the way around us. Now we are going to meet our energetic boundaries.

Perceive the sphere that is about arms length from your body in all directions. Not only is it the brain-mapped edge, it is also your energy boundary. You can envision it in whatever color suits you, but see it as just as thick and real as the proprioceptive boundaries. What's inside this sphere is you. What's outside it is not you. The space is filled with your life force energy moving within you. It is your beliefs, your consciousness, and your ancestry. It is all the intangible things that make up who you are.

The first part of this exercise is to play with the size of the sphere. We cannot change our physical boundaries, or the edges that our brain takes into account, but we can move our energy. Allow your energy to expand slowly, taking in the furniture you are sitting on, the floor, the other furniture in the room, the height of the ceiling, all the way out to the walls of the room. Take a breath here. Notice the sensation of having your energy filling the room. What sensations do you have?

Then bring your energy back closer to your body, releasing the objects in the room from your awareness, coming back to the bubble that is arms length all the way around you.

Now bring your energy in closer... to your skin. Notice your skin as the boundary of your body. And then pull your energy in even closer. Pull your awareness all the way to your bones, to your core. Take a breath there and notice what it feels like to have your attention pointed to your deep center.

Let your energy expand back to arms length again. Bring back the image of drawing this boundary in the air. Feel how solid and real that edge feels. Now just give yourself a moment to observe that boundary.

Things you may notice: What color is it? How solid does it seem? Are there holes in it? Does some part of it feel thicker or thinner? Can you sense the arms length boundary behind you? Under your feet?

ISLAND MOTHER

Nothing is more lonely than living in your body not knowing who you are.

~ Island Mother

Inquire
Within, Self-
Determination
~ Island Mother

THE ISLAND LANDSCAPE

There is more diversity among islands than you might think at first pass. The major characteristics of an island are how it came to be, how far it is from land, its size, and where it is in the world. Some are covered in ice and some are in temperate areas, but tropical islands are probably most iconic.

The farther an island is from another land mass, the more likely it is to have unique species. In other words, the more distance and time the island has been isolated, the more it develops its own flora and fauna. You might say that an island becomes its unique self the longer it is apart and the less influence other lands have on it.

While the island is isolated from other land masses, it is deeply intimate with the ocean. Sea temperature, waves, and salty air all influence island geography as well as the plants and animals that live there. People who live on islands are often well versed in the ways of the ocean, its currents, animals, and the way the weather meets the land.

ISLAND MOTHER

The obvious feature of Island Mother is that she is alone, standing singly in a vast ocean. Sometimes others are near her, but she is fundamentally on her own. Our individuality, our ability to know ourselves and stand for our right to be as we are, allows us to develop and solidify a sense of self. Claiming our individuality often plays out on the continuum between our feelings of solitude versus isolation. The strength of our individuality is connected to a sense of solitude, whereas isolation can feel like rejection or abandonment.

The irony for Island Mother is that our sense of self is rooted in having received something psychologists call "unconditional positive regard", which usually comes from someone else. Unconditional positive regard is the reflection that we are inherently accepted and supported without having to do or be anything in particular to earn it. Ideally, this comes from our first caregiver(s) when we are very young. It instills the foundational worth on which we build our sense of self.

As we grow up, our sense of self develops, through internal reflection and choice. Solitude is important, because when we are alone and quiet, we can hear what is true upwelling from within. The beginnings of positive regard come from external sources, but as we grow, spending quiet time with our own heart and mind further develops and nurtures internal personal regard and a strong sense of self. In effect, we are creating a nurturing and protective inner adult.

Without early support for positive self development, isolation can worsen and reinforce a negative sense of self. This can lead to depression, feelings of low self-worth, and poor boundaries. Instead of solitude that feeds self-awareness, we feel isolated and neglected. Island Mother's primary job is to restore her sense of self through interactions that confirm her inherent value as a person, which she often affords to others, but not herself.

If positive regard was lacking for you in some way, know that all is not lost. The island is surrounded by the ocean, which is the origin of all life. The womb, the container, the possibility, is present. The island rises as a mountain from the waters, taking a stand for who you are. You and the landscapes can work together to recreate what was missing in the past. Today you can cultivate the regard and positive sense of self that you were not given, if this is a difficulty you faced.

STRENGTHS OF ISLAND MOTHER

Island Mother can be significantly impacted by childhood wounds of rejection and abandonment. The pain of isolation can make her wary of others and fearful of connection. But she also brings the possibility for renewal and redefinition. We are always defining and refining who we are, who we want to be, and how we express ourselves. Island Mother's work is always present.

At her best, Island Mother considers herself worthy of her own attention and care. She feels most comfortable in her own space, in her own company, and values stability, slowness, deep awareness, and solitude. She may identify as an introvert, an empath, a highly sensitive person, or some combination of those.

The strengths of Island Mother come from two sources. One is that she is embedded in the ocean, and thus has a built-in connection with the source of all life. Possibility for further refinement is inherently available. The other source of Island Mother's strength is that in many ways she is a mountain standing in the sea. She can be formidable and strong in the face of difficulty.

As we develop our internal Island Mother, we deeply sense and feel the support of the ocean—the feeling that depth and breadth are both possible. Island Mother has access to an easy inner sense of spirituality, which brings with it the ability to tap into the deep and wide nature of our inner world. Island Mother has a strong foundation for self-determination, even if there was no support for its expression in her early life.

Island Mother is deeply embedded in the spiritual and internal world, giving her the reflection skills and self-awareness that she needs to know herself well. When she builds on awareness of herself with self-compassion and kindness, she develops a strength of character that arises from within. She is not only able to see herself clearly, but she has cultivated the positive inner sense of self needed for a strong internal guidance system.

As a result of her spiritually grounded, self-reflective orientation, Island Mother's self-care practices are pristine. She defines, reflects, and embodies what is hers, and doesn't pretend at what is not. In her best moments, she can be secure in her own gifts and let others do what is theirs to do without any jealousy or competition.

Her internal security depends on tending and nourishing her self and her gifts. This is not the kind of self-care that is embedded inside of cultural expectations or determined by your economic status. This is the kind of self-care that comes from a deep tending to your core, that arises from your needs and pleasures. The goal of this kind of self-care is body and soul nourishment.

Island Mother has a strong inner center and wants to support that trait in those around her. She utilizes her internal guidance system to make time and space for herself and those who are important to her. Deep and active listening is one of her core skills. She is sensitive and empathetic, often hearing the request under the demand, especially of her children.

The delicate balance between the strengths and struggles of Island Mother are played out in the continuum between solitude and isolation. Island Mother when she feels resourced, is likely to choose solitude because it supports her inner sense-abilities and her spiritual practice. Island Mother, when depleted, will be prone to depression and isolation out of fear and self-loathing.

STRUGGLES OF ISLAND MOTHER

To be an island is to have no dependable connections. This can lead to isolation and fracturing of the sense of self. Being a human island means either being literally alone, or more likely, it means that we present an external persona that is totally different than how we feel or look to ourselves on the inside. This "being two people" is difficult and dismissive of our needs, and it often leads to anxiety and depression.

Island Mother is perhaps the mother most likely to feel like she has to do everything herself. She may self-isolate because there are cultural norms she knows she struggles to meet, or she fears she cannot perform to expectations. She might be afraid of how others would view her if they knew her struggles, and so in an act of self-protection she goes it alone.

While, to some degree, all of the Mothers are prone to feeling like they don't belong, it is Island Mother who grapples most with the conscious realization of needing both a sense of self and a sense of belonging in her community. She sees belonging through the lens of her individual self. That is, she wonders who she is and what she provides to her relationships. She wants to know how she fits into her community through being true to herself.

A very common expression of Island Mother might be depression—the result of a lack of a sense of self and a twisted message about her own lovability, capability, and importance stemming from abuse and/or neglect. This internal devaluing of her own experience and needs leaves her hardly knowing how to relate to others. She might also feel that other people are dangerous and require her to expend so much psychic protection energy that she simply chooses not to engage with others.

Island Mother has few people she feels are close enough to call *real* friends. She may have many people around her, but unless she feels safe, she will not be truly vulnerable within these friendships. Interactions with friends might be centered on intellectual ideas, projects, or interests rather than in a sense of identity or life purpose. Island Mother may feel most comfortable with friendships that have a shared, stable context. The reason for a gathering would hold the relationships if she was afraid that her presence wasn't enough. Anything she does that is deeply personal, like her spiritual practice, is most likely private and solitary.

Island Mother may struggle to recognize the influence of the environment or past experience. She is often so tightly aware of her own sensory experience that she might not see the influence of oppression, control, or trauma on her present sense of herself.

When she prioritizes others' perspectives over her own, she may take too much responsibility for her own situation, seeing any conflict as evidence of her personal failures. She is prone to self-blame rather than holding others accountable for their behaviors.

Remember that a healthy sense of self is predicated on receiving some kind of unconditional positive regard as a child. Island Mother's innate capabilities are completely undermined by not having a reflection of herself as strong and capable from a childhood caregiver. When a heavily negative sense of self is created, the result is a deeply harmful inner critic and panic-level fear of further rejection.

This is tricky territory, as it requires both an external source of unconditional positive regard and the restoration of a protective and nourishing inner voice. If Island Mother feels depleted, she might feel she wants someone to help. Unfortunately, in a culture of individualism, someone in this circumstance is often told that she's acting like a "victim." Furthermore, she'll be told that it's her responsibility to love and regard herself before anyone else can see her as good or worthy.

It is impossible to magically think positively about yourself after years of being told otherwise. An inner critic embedded in early childhood experiences of poor regard cannot just change its character because you say so. Evidence of lovability and acceptability will have to be found. This requires interaction with the environment and other living beings to create the protective and nourishing inner voice. This can be done in relationship with the Earth as a proxy for the loving caregiver.

ISLAND MOTHER IN PARENTING

The resourced Island Mother has a deep inner well of Self, and she is good at supporting emotional intelligence and caring in her children. She has a natural tendency to encourage the development of strong autonomy, as well as empathy. She overlaps some with Desert Mother here, in riding the line between wanting her kids to have independence and offering them support and guidance. The special offering of Island Mother, though, is acceptance of who her children are at their core and development of their own inner strengths, regardless of their level of independence.

If depleted or depressed, Island Mother might drop the ball completely as she gets absorbed in her inner workings. Or she might use her inner workings to attempt to solve all of her problems, instead of reaching out toward those close to her. That is, she may resort to believing in all of her internal conclusions without checking her perceptions with the outside world. This is often the basis of conflict between Island Mother and her family and friends. She interprets connections between multiple events that others don't perceive or did not intend. She may have a tendency to project these stories on others.

Island Mother's children will likely lean one of two ways along a continuum. One way is that her children will feel free and independent with a strong sense of what they want and need. They'll know themselves well and base their choices easily on their sense of knowing what is right for them. The other possibility is that children may be disappointed by Island Mother's lack of attention. They might feel isolated and abandoned, creating a negative inner critic, and will grow up with a tendency to abandon themselves when their needs inevitably arise. Where children and mothers end up on this continuum depends primarily on the constitution of the child and how present and responsive Island Mother can be.

These inner world stories either form loops that keep us stuck and unable to make significant movement, or they get transferred to the intellect and become disconnected from the lived experience that follows. Often, I suspect, it's some combination. At least, I have personally expressed both of these routes. On one hand we have the expression of a "collapsed mother," and on the other hand we have an "intellectual mother." This translates into a wide range of possible Island Mother expressions.

Island Mother is also about how we follow our gut / heart / instinct. She's about using pleasure and rest as guidance for what to do next, instead of criticism and "getting with the program." Island Mother invites us to come back to ourselves and let our next move upwell from within instead of gauging what we "should" do from outside of us.

If we were supported in listening to ourselves when we were young, we might feel that we were already living true to ourselves before having our own children, and we may not feel so lost in motherhood. When we do not receive support for being self-reflective and are constantly drawn to look outside of ourselves for our well-being, then we might not realize that we don't know our own hearts until we're deep in the struggles of raising our own children. It seems common among women I've talked to for this awareness to come in their 40s.

THE INNATE GIFT OF ISLAND MOTHER

Island Mother's gift is solitude. It is the reclamation of isolation and loneliness that has enough space for Island Mother to begin to see and tend to herself. In solitude, she grows her inner capacities true to her nature. She becomes self-determined and clear. Island Mother is the hearth goddess of her inner world. Her superpower is the ability to deeply and meaningfully nourish and protect this inner world—an ability we might also call self-care.

In more concrete terms, solitude is a capacity to be with yourself as you might be with a friend. The inner experience in which we get to know ourselves *as* ourselves... not as extensions of our families, churches, sports teams, or whatever other groups with which we might identify. In solitude, the perspectives of ourselves that are given to us by these groups fall away. We find out what is needed and wanted to truly care for our inner world.

Simply looking inside isn't enough, though. It is only the beginning. When we first look inside, we find things we don't really want to see—things that bring us pain and cause us to dislike ourselves. This is what pushes Island Mother toward isolation. Her inherent comfort with turning inward due to her introverted nature creates a double inward spiral that may result in her collapse. The gift of solitude, of getting comfortable with oneself, is not available, and instead she falls into despair.

If we can keep moving around the Landscape, cultivating the tools and gifts of all of the Mothers, Island Mother eventually finds her autonomous and true Self. She finds her well of compassion, vulnerable humanity, and unconditional love when she looks to herself. This is her power place, as it's from here that profound relationships of connection are made. When we look inside and find ourselves worthy of love and hope and joy, we more easily create healthy relationships that sustain us rather than drain us.

CULTIVATING ISLAND MOTHER

Body-centered practices can help us integrate how we think and how we experience this work. Through our body experience we get a deeper knowing and understanding. The following activities are suggestions for how you might begin to interact with Island Mother in addition to your reading.

The Island Mother Question: Who am I?

Island Mother Activity

This is a meditation, or inner exploration, of your unique vibration. I call it your Cellular Song. The most necessary thing is a quiet place. You'll need about 10 uninterrupted minutes for this inner journey.

Begin by closing your eyes and allowing things to settle within you. The goal here is to give yourself the space to feel into the invitations.

Take three breaths as you allow yourself to set down your worries, and the hurry of so much to do. Allow your muscles to release the sense of urgency that pushes you through your day. You can pick all these things up again later if they're serving you. In this moment, give yourself fully to relaxation.

Notice your breath. Notice the muscles in your feet, legs, belly, back, arms, shoulders, neck, and face. Use your breath to consciously release any tension in your body that isn't about holding you upright. How relaxed can you get?

Turn your attention to your heartbeat. Because you are relaxed, you may not be able to feel it beat for beat, but get in touch with how it's in there, keeping a rhythm for you. Without thinking too hard, just allow for the fact that blood is flowing through your arteries and veins. Cells are picking up nutrients from and discarding unnecessary items to the blood. This exchange is happening in a pattern, with a rhythm. Release any thoughts about the mechanics of it all, and tune into the song that is emerging. The heartbeat and the breath form the basic beat. The melody is made of the movement of nutrients across membranes, and the hum of the fluid moving through vessels forms a harmony.

This song is uniquely you. It is your body and system working at your well-being and vitality. It is the motion of your inner landscape. It is lively and vibrant in you. There is nothing you have to do, no way you have to be for this to be true. It's true for all of us. It is something we share, though our cellular songs will differ.

Following your awareness to your cellular song can be helpful in times when you're feeling uncertain of what comes next, or what you should do in a particular situation. It returns you to your own sovereignty, your own heart, your own needs. Acting from here ensures that any steps taken include kindness and compassion for yourself.

Going Deeper with Island Mother

To go deeper we build on our new relationship with our Cellular Song. In relationship, we begin with an introduction (which we just did), and then the relationship grows through interaction. One way to be with your Cellular Song is to use your voice to relate back to it. You can sing or hum.

Humming, singing, and using our voice in a soothing way directly activates the vagus nerve, which perceives the voice vibration as a calming sort of activity. When this part of the nervous system is activated, we feel relaxed, soothed, and easygoing. This is why mothers for all time and all over the world sing and hum to babies. It is a simple, elegant, and effective calming tool, not only for small children but for all of us.

Sit on the edge of your chair, or on a hard-enough chair or couch that you can sit up on your sitz bones, nice and straight. The goal is to find a position in which you're upright and your belly has plenty of space (that is, you're not hunched over your belly). Take a deep breath in, aiming to release enough of the tension at the low back, the pelvic floor, and the front of the belly, to breathe in a nice full breath. Exhale completely. Take another breath in, and this time, hum on the exhale.

For a hum that really reaches the vagus nerve at the back of the throat area, you'll want to hold your mouth as if you have a precious egg inside and you don't want to break it. Your lips will be held together gently, the roof of your mouth will feel lifted, like the curved ceiling of a cathedral (or as if it's lifted to make room for that egg you are imagining in there). Your tongue will lay at the bottom of your mouth, mostly relaxed, or a tiny bit like a little bowl (holding that egg again!). Neither push the air out of the hum, nor hold it back. Let it release naturally. Repeat two more times for a total of three hums. Now notice how you feel.

There are many vocal practices that utilize humming or chanting as regulatory and spiritual tools. If this feels really good to you, I highly recommend looking around for more structure around these practices that allow you to feel held. Alternatively, if this is enough, that's awesome, too.

MOUNTAIN MOTHER

Come when it's time to rest. Come when you need to be held.

~ Mountain Mother

Deep sigh
I fall in
Sync with her heartbeat
~ Mountain Mother

THE MOUNTAIN LANDSCAPE

Mountain landscapes are tall and sometimes formidable. They feel sturdy and powerful, like they'll stand the test of time. In some traditions mountains are seen as the places from which we can touch Spirit.

Mountains have a strong and stable presence. They change a landscape from stretching horizontally to reaching skyward, as if dramatically shifting our perspective lest we forget where we're really going.

The idea of scaling mountains evokes a sense of grandiosity. It is also a metaphor for meeting challenges in life head on. Sometimes that means making a massive effort and stepping forward, and sometimes it means simply meeting each day, doing the next necessary thing until we get through. Either way, the solidity of rock, the presence of the mountain, the imagery of climbing, all beckon us to keep moving forward.

Mountains and their enduring presence help us take the long view and see the benefits of slow progress. They are here for the long haul, persistent and still. While mountains invite us to be mindful of the present moment, they are also good reminders to look at the bigger picture. Mountains encourage us both to keep our attention here in this moment and to consider what we want our legacy to be.

MOUNTAIN MOTHER

Mountain Mother is solid and dependable. You will always find her where you expect her. She is always available to hold you, and to hold all of the things that feel too much for you to hold alone. She is calm and cool, and it feels like she's right here with you.

Really, what Mountain Mother has is presence. She has a way of being still in the face of upheaval that leaves you feeling protected. She listens deeply, without judgment and with spaciousness in her attention. Her presence holds you and makes you feel seen, heard, and understood.

In psychology terms we would say that our secure attachment comes from Mountain Mother. She is the one who makes us feel comforted. She calms our nervous system. She makes us feel safe. She is the one who soothes.

Mountain Mother is deeply grounded. She's an anchor, trustworthy and predictable. However, while the term "grounded" is common, I prefer "settled" because it feels more accurate to me. "Settled" points to one of those "missing skills" that result from enduring harmful parenting: we still need to learn to calm our nervous system. We can imagine growing roots into the ground as much as we want (a common grounding technique), but if we don't learn to stop... and breathe... and settle our nervous system, then "grounding" can be just a mental exercise that makes us think we should feel better.

When we talk about settling, there is a situational type and a foundational type. The situational type of settling is about re-regulating our nervous systems after a surprise or shock. It addresses a temporary dysregulation. In certain situations where re-regulating doesn't occur, the problem can get locked in and become a foundational type of dysregulation.

Foundational dysregulation results when we accumulate unresolved situational experiences and become stuck—this circulates a high level of stress though our bodies constantly. Common indications of foundational dysregulation are hypervigilance and chronic anxiety.

Mountain Mother can help us find the ground in both of these states, but they involve slightly different skills. In situational settling we can use tools like breathing exercises, settling imagery, or some types of movement practice (putting our hands on our heart or stomach, qi gong, tai chi, yoga, etc.). If we need connection in order to settle, we can talk briefly with a friend, recounting and reprocessing the upsetting event.

Foundational settling requires that we know a bit about how our nervous system works more fundamentally. This is also the kind of settling that we unconsciously model after our childhood caregivers. We learn to respond to stress as they did, and we build our nervous system function off of theirs. This retraining of the nervous system is a commitment. The best way I've found to do this is to make small commitments to settling my system multiple times a day. I have practices for morning and evening, and some that I sprinkle throughout the day depending on what I need.

Mountain Mother is a perfect ally for this work. She is dependable, present, and reassuring. And this work is about creating that kind of physical, mental, and emotional safety in our own nervous systems. Mountain Mother holds the tools we need to cultivate the practices of well-being.

STRENGTHS OF MOUNTAIN MOTHER

Mountain Mother is naturally good at settling herself and connecting with people around her. She doesn't really have to think about it. Her mere presence puts people at ease and gets them in touch with their feelings of rootedness and solidity. Her soft and subtle murmur is "you are right here, right now." When she says that, we feel ourselves settle into our feet. We inhabit our bodies a little more, and our minds grow calm. She is gentle, quiet, unassuming. She feels like coming home.

Her listening skills are so much more than just hearing you. She practices a whole-body receiving of all levels of communication. Mountain Mother watches, listens, senses, moves with you. She makes you feel not only understood, but reflected. She hears so deeply that it's like gentle waves conveying your essence to hers and reflecting back again.

Mountain Mother gives us the feeling that we're being received with presence and gentleness. With her nearby we feel safe and steady, as if nothing can shake us. She makes us feel like we can live a life true to ourselves with permission to know our own hearts and to tend to them. Mountain Mother is willing to own her feelings and take a stand from her felt sense of herself. From here she is connected and certain.

She is the one who stands for truth and never wavers. She is committed to what is before her, as it is, in all of its complexity and wildness. Mountain Mother has the compassion, trust, and persistence needed for the long haul. She inspires her children to be true to themselves, and she lives up to this value for herself.

Mountain Mother provides unconditional positive regard. She receives us as we are, with respect and openness. When we receive positive regard from our caregivers, it lets us know that we don't have to live up to someone else's standard to be loved—we just are. *We are okay as we are and don't need to change in order to be valued by someone else.* This is how we learn self-acceptance. If we struggle with this, it's often because we did not get this kind of reception as children. Mountain Mother is here to hold us in that positive regard so we can find our self-acceptance and self-determination.

STRUGGLES OF MOUNTAIN MOTHER

Because she has a penchant for slowness and stillness, Mountain Mother runs the risk of staying too long in one place. She might choose to stay in a lonely marriage too long, delaying her needs and gratifications for so long that she forgets that she even has her own desires. She is the one most likely to give up her energy to feed others, even when they're grown and ready to become independent.

A woman that spends a lot of time in Mountain Mother energy might want to hold onto her children and keep them from leaving home. Her secret hope is that they remain close to her—that they never grow up and go live their own lives, but that they settle down into her realm and are lifelong friends. Mountain Mother's gift for attachment can turn too close, too dependent.

This could also contribute to martyrdom in Mountain Mother. If she builds resentment about giving continuously, always being there when her child needs her, she may become manipulative in order to keep that sense of closeness. The child either falls into codependency or rebels against the tethers. Mountain Mother may struggle with "rebellious teens." It makes sense, as teenagers are developmentally trying on the possibility of being their own person apart from their family of origin. This would make Mountain Mother wring her hands in distress.

I am not suggesting that teen rebellion is the mother's fault. However, given a dynamic of a struggling Mountain Mother and a rebellious child, it is worth taking a look at where a shift in approach could open a different way of relating with one another. The teenager is not in a developmental position to come up with a creative solution to this deeply complex relationship, so it is the parent's job to work toward that. It's possible that encouraging curiosity in the teen's world and following some of their enthusiasm for newness and exploration could even be medicine for Mountain Mother herself.

MOUNTAIN MOTHER IN PARENTING

The challenge of Mountain Mother is to support her children into being their own people without dictating who she wants them to be. It is hard for Mountain Mother to let go. But once she hones that skill, she becomes a grounded and safe place to return to... always.

If we are lucky enough to have parents who encourage us in the direction of our hearts, rather than in the direction of "what we are supposed to do" or what they expect us to do, then maybe we already have the tools we need to find our whole selves again. We don't have to "get with the program." We can live our own lives.

If, instead, we were told that getting a job and paying bills was of primary importance—or getting married and having kids, or any other societal expectation—we might never have had an opportunity to think about what we want. We did what was expected of us. Then when the moment comes when we wonder what we're doing in this world, there is no answer, no "before kids" self to reference, and we are now exhausted *and* trying to find our true personal passion.

Stability is key for Mountain Mother. For me, the desire for stability and safety came from childhood trauma. I didn't know anyone like Mountain Mother. No one stood for me. The child-rearing wisdom of the 1970s had a lot of "let kids figure it out on their own" attitude, even when acts of violence were repeated over and over. Children that don't receive Mountain Mother nourishment might feel adrift, abandoned, or alone.

My own inner Mountain Mother grew out of the wounds I had around this. It took me a long time to learn to take a stand for myself, but when I became a mother I found that standing for my kids came easily. This is where I met my "mother intuition."

I was still working on my PhD when my eldest daughter was born. I was sure I was smart enough to be a mom, but I had no idea how different academic smarts were from intuitive ones. When she was about 5 months old, she started waking up screaming every 30-45 minutes. All day. All night. Neither of us slept. She was clearly in pain, but I didn't know why. I took her to the pediatrician several times, who repeatedly told me she didn't think anything was wrong. I pressed for help. Finally, in total exasperation, she referred us to a pediatric gastroenterologist, who confirmed that what was happening wasn't normal and was able to help us. I advocated for my baby from the basis of my intuition (and desperation), and we were able to resolve the problem. It was new ground for me in many ways, and the experience anchored my sense of trusting in my gut feelings or "just knowing"... my intuition.

THE INNATE GIFT OF MOUNTAIN MOTHER

Mountain Mother finds it easy to be totally present with what is. She does this through cultivating her attention and awareness. On the outside she appears solid, centered, and strong. On the inside she is grounded and settled. In her book *Reclaiming the Wild Soul*, Mary Reynolds Thompson reflects this sense of anchoring and security when she says that mountains are "the bones of the Earth."

The sensations we have in response to our natural surroundings isn't new. I suspect this sense of the earth as solid and enduring is a widely held feeling across time and place. I think of the great stones carved from mountainsides that have been used across the planet for megalithic sites like Stonehenge in England, Adam's Calendar in South Africa, or Jungnim-ri Dolmens in South Korea. These creations occur on every major continent in the world. I can only imagine that the people who placed them felt they were stable and lasting, and that was part of why they would do the work of creating them.

Mountain Mother expresses her gifts of security, strength, and endurance through presence. Her greatest skill is her ability to listen—to truly hear and reflect back—giving people a sense that she understands them and is giving them her full attention.

She brings her whole self to tasks, as well. She can be truly present, even when washing dishes, tending to tired children, or recognizing and dealing with her own wounds. She doesn't run away or avoid. She uses her steadiness to bring what she can offer to the situation. At her best she tempers this non-avoidance with knowing that she can't fix everything. She remembers that being side by side with someone is soothing in itself.

Mountain Mother also has a tension within her between being present in the here and now, and her naturally enduring nature. She beckons us not only to be mindful of this moment, but also to keep our legacy in mind over the long haul. She is deeply aware that this moment is embedded in unfolding time. That is, this moment is not to be experienced in isolation of other moments, but as a continuous path that has a context of past moments, and is full of possibility through future decision making.

The bottom line is that Mountain Mother stands for the existence of our innate Body Wisdom. This is the idea that we have not only intellectual knowledge, but embodied knowledge. Mountain Mother invites us into these aspects of ourselves—into a totally different orientation. These are often the parts of us that we hoped were there, but we doubted because of things others told us. Our embodied understanding moves us from seeing our struggles as evidence that we are broken and wrong, into seeing struggle as a way to our inner guidance and wisdom. Embodied knowledge orients us toward seeing what is good and right about ourselves.

In our bodies, this sense of settling, and the orientation that we can know ourselves through being present, helps us stand tall, with our shoulders relaxed. Being settled or grounded is the foundation of dignity. When we are grounded we are right here right now, accepting of what is and willing to stand for what needs to be.

CULTIVATING MOUNTAIN MOTHER

Mountain Mother naturally tends toward following her body wisdom. Finding a somatic experience of her gifts helps us know her better. The following activities are suggestions for how you might begin to interact with Mountain Mother through your body to further develop the skills she offers.

The Mountain Mother Question: What am I committed to?
(How can I tend to my own care, security, and stability?)

Mountain Mother Activity

Find a quiet and comfortable place where you won't be interrupted for about 10 minutes. Invite your mind to begin to relax. If it helps, you can imagine the energy in your head melting, and then running down your face, neck, shoulders, and arms. You can pick up your thoughts again later.

Trace your spine down to your tailbone. Feel your body in contact with the furniture or the ground. Let yourself relax further into being held and supported. Notice that as your physical body presses down on earth, that the earth energy is also rising up to meet you. You are supported, met, exactly. Tap into that energy coming toward you from the earth below you. Notice its quality. Steady... present... even. Allow your nervous system to receive this experience fully. Let it help repair some of the ways that you were surprised, neglected, or disregarded in the past. Let the consistency and the presence of the earth below you offer your nervous system a steady and stable experience in this moment.

You can carry this sense of settledness with you all of the time. And when you forget or a stressor comes up, remember that the earth is always right here under your feet to remember with you.

Going Deeper with Mountain Mother

I have had to consciously learn Mountain Mother skills. I've found that it helps me if I move slower and try to make more space in my calendar. I've had to embrace being an introvert, to learn to say "no" to the things I don't really want to do, and which take too much of my energy. I've also committed to saying "yes" to my kids as much as I can whenever they're asking for time with me. I've cultivated the muscle of noticing when my kids need me to be present to them, and when they're tired, overwhelmed, hungry, or sad.

I try to organize my work schedule so that when I'm with my kids they truly have my attention. I've had to recommit to that over and over, because it's so easy to follow inspiration, social media, or the metaphorical "shiny object." Recommitting is a Mountain Mother process. For some it comes easy; for some it doesn't. In our current Western culture I imagine it doesn't come easy for most of us-it's much easier and more acceptable to be distracted and busy.

Take a look at your calendar. What can you let go? What time do you need to protect for yourself and your children? What stands in the way of the clear expression of your presence?

Commitment to our values means we have to take action and protect our time and energy. So, as good as it feels to take a moment and settle into our relationship with Earth, soil, and Mountain Mother, it also takes continuous commitment on our part to arrange ourselves in alignment with what works for us.

RIVER MOTHER

May your path be clear and easy. May you be successful and prosperous.

~ River Mother

Focus
On the means
And the arrival
~ River Mother

THE RIVER LANDSCAPE

Rivers are landscapes of moving water—sometimes fast and direct within their banks, and sometimes slower and more meandering, but always headed to a gathering place. The waters of rivers dig deep into rock and dirt to form pathways to an ocean or lake. While their pace is variable, their direction is not. Water is always headed downhill with an intrinsic determination.

Water itself is the element of life. This planet could still have rocks and minerals and wind, but without water there would be no life. It is a pliable element, moving around harder surfaces, but capable of sculpting even the hardest of them over time. Water is persistent and insistent, always moving toward the ocean.

River systems are in complex relationships with the environment around them. River flow and route are influenced by the animals, plants, and humans that surround them. They are interconnected and interdependent.

Many rivers have been altered from their natural flow by dams, either to serve as a power source or to create reservoirs. Human use of waterways has fundamentally altered many of them such that the water no longer flows all the way to its destination.

RIVER MOTHER

River Mother is a gatherer at heart. Each small tributary coming from the mountains feeds into her. She has, in the waters that flow to her, tiny tidbits of minerals, parts of Mountain Mother with seeds of the trueness of her course. She knows her own strength, and she is aware of the strengths of others. River Mother is good at organizing the household and people, creating plans and schedules to get done what needs to be done.

She is persistent and single-minded in her focus on the tasks of mothering. She doesn't always leave enough room for rest or differing opinions. She has the direction, focus and constant forward momentum to make sure that everyone gets where they need to go. Everyone gets their needs met, and the structure of the family is well served.

River Mother is good at observing and pays a great deal of attention to details. She notices what needs attention or fixing. She is efficient and prudent. She can predict needs and desires and is on top of the happenings of daily life. A little effort spent setting expectations and monitoring the situation allows her to head off trouble with ease.

Add her love of detail to the variability of her pace, and you can see how she creates magic. She can be focused and rushing, and she can also be slow and gentle. Eddies give us places to rest, notice what is happening, and not move on too quickly. With a force of will behind her, she is phenomenal at getting things accomplished.

STRENGTHS OF RIVER MOTHER

At her best, River Mother is highly efficient and makes space and time for her children, partner (if she has one), and friends. When she is willing to make room for open play, connection, and rest, she is a marvelous mother who seems to have it all together. She finds a way to balance her needs and those of her family. This really hinges on the ability to not overschedule.

From my observations, many women strive to be River Mother. She is in motion, which our culture values highly. She is productive—you can see and measure what she's accomplished. She does all the background work to make sure that her family is able to go to school, work, and out into the world with full bellies and clean clothes. River Mother is highly prized and seen as an ideal mother in our culture. She does everything and looks happy about it.

She has masterful management skills, so when she's at her best everyone feels tended to, noticed, and provided for. River Mother has each need broken down into its component parts, and tasks organized to support those needs. Each gets its turn to be addressed, but none is allowed to take up too much room or energy.

River Mother is also good at keeping up with change. She's on top of the next need or upcoming issue. She can predict and manage what's ahead. She carries the bulk of the mental load of running the household and being responsible for the whole family. Because of her efficiency, these jobs may fall easily in her natural territory.

River Mother is most comfortable keeping everything and everyone in rhythm together. She tends well to the details while also holding the bigger picture of family and relationships. She prioritizes the tasks of maintaining her house and family activities because it keeps everyone together and feeling comfortable and at ease.

STRUGGLES OF RIVER MOTHER

For many, though, holding the movement and direction of the whole family fails to live up to its pretty veneer. Unless parenting was a focal desire in life, and you find joy in the tasks of running a household, it may be hard to feel in sync with the strengths of River Mother. Unappreciated emotional labor takes a huge toll on a relationship, most likely between partnered adults raising children. The primary caregiver may begin to feel used, underacknowledged, and like no one cares if they're even around.

A depleted River Mother can get so focused on organizing (or controlling) other people and events that she forgets to leave room for them to be who they are. For children, this can be very difficult if they don't get to express their own wishes and thoughts, or follow their own preferences. A depleted River Mother may resort to shaming in order to get quick compliance from her children. After all, her priority is movement toward the vision, not giving people space to be who they are.

River Mother doesn't always make enough room for the opinions and needs of others if she did not expect and plan for them. She might be inflexible, with a "my way or the highway" approach. Her house is her own, and she knows how she wants it. The expectation is that others conform to that vision. What doesn't fit that expectation might not get attention, even if it's truly warranted and needed.

She might struggle to leave herself enough time, getting swept up in the busyness involved in maintaining her own work, while caring for other family members, home, and children. In this case, the time left when the tasks are done may not be enough. She is too willing to put social events, friends, and partners/lovers ahead of taking time to restore herself. This drains River Mother, and she may slow to a trickle and not have enough of herself to nourish anyone else. This can become frustrating and exhausting, feeding the inner critic that suggests she isn't enough, isn't doing enough, isn't providing enough. Adding this strain to her depletion can lead her into the realm of Desert Mother.

A depleted River Mother's emotional landing place might be resentment and overwhelm. If she spends all of her time organizing and doing the emotional labor of her family, she might find herself underappreciated, giving energy to others and not finding enough energy or appreciation to fuel herself. Clearly this isn't sustainable. Thus, she might feel depleted, exhausted, and overwhelmed.

RIVER MOTHER IN PARENTING

As a parent, River Mother has a tendency toward being busy and highly organized. At her best, she makes her children feel cared for and held. Things are often in motion—opportunities are everywhere for meeting new people and experiencing new things. A strong and happy River Mother and an extroverted child are a very good match. They appreciate each other's styles and enjoy the opportunities that arise from their interplay.

Some children could find an active schedule difficult, as there is little room left to explore their own desires and hearts. They don't have enough unstructured time to learn to be bored, to entertain themselves, or to be still and thoughtful and contemplative. All of those things require spaciousness of time and attention.

Even a well-balanced River Mother could be overwhelming for a child with introvert tendencies. This brings to our attention how it's not the mother being good or bad, or the child being good or bad, but whether their innate tendencies are a good match. This is true in most relationships. When it feels like a struggle, and the other person isn't doing what we hoped or wanted, it isn't that the people are bad or wrong. The difficulty is that one person's offering and the needs of the other are simply mismatched.

Because she is of the waters, River Mother can be reflective and thoughtful as well as efficient and productive. She has the tools to teach her children to balance the inner world with the outer, their thoughts and visions with the tangible expressions of their values. She is the place where hope and possibility meet action and movement. When she's clear on what she wants, it's easy enough to make it happen.

I have to admit, this is so not me. I felt more like motherhood pulled me along kicking and screaming, and less that I floated down the river with ease on an innertube guided by the clearly defined banks of the river. Luckily, early in motherhood, I made friends with a couple of good River Mothers who taught me what I do know about this archetype. Basically, I recognized them as having parenting skills I didn't have, and emulated them. The River Mothers I know had clear values and expectations of themselves and their children. They had all of the certainty I felt I lacked.

THE INNATE GIFT OF RIVER MOTHER

River Mother cultivates a deep relationship with her purpose. I think the expression of purpose is made of one part persistence and one part surrender, with an anchor in your values. Once in place, a sense of purpose gives meaning to life.

Purpose is more than your job or role. It is your way of being and living on the planet. As we consider River Mother, keep in mind that your purpose need not be defined by what you do for others, or what you accomplish in a day, or your obligations. What if purpose is so much more? What if it is about values, as well as action? What if it is about meaning, as well as outcome?

What if we dive into the meaning (that we sourced from hanging out with Island Mother) under what we are doing. It joins questions such as "why did I want to be a parent?" with "what do I want to teach my children about being human"? It combines the value with the action.

River Mother benefits from being crystal clear about what she is cultivating and what she wants to leave as her legacy. She has the focus and drive to make anything happen, but if she isn't clear about where she wants to go, her potential dissipates and she falls easily into busyness. A River Mother who is capable of waiting and being still gains much in clarity of purpose. She can be a quality leader when she achieves harmony between her natural River Mother drive and her ability to be still (Mountain Mother) in order to tap into her own knowing (Island Mother) and make space for creativity and whimsy (Wind Mother).

When River Mother is struggling she becomes frustrated, impatient, and resentful that her plans don't work more easily. She might know what she wants in the moment, but it's good for her to sit back every so often and check in with where she's going. Are the things she's doing getting the results she desires? If not, what other approach could she take? Is it about the timing? Is it being rushed or held back? Is this plan working for everyone it impacts? If not, what adjustments might be needed?

Purpose is created from a combination of persistence and surrender. Persistence is a good tool for critical situations, and qualities or processes we highly value. It is what brings together the life force energy needed for accomplishment. Surrender is for the clutter. It's for what stands in the way of what is important to us. River Mother rushes over rocks and carves deep canyons from persistence. She also slows and circles back on herself in the eddies, making sure she's true to her purpose.

CULTIVATING THE RIVER MOTHER

Somatic practices can help us find a new way to perceive new information. Through our bodies, we can feel resonance or dissonance. These sensations can help guide us when we don't know what else to do. The following activities are suggestions for experiencing River Mother.

The River Mother Question: Where do I want to go?

River Mother Activity

After years of observing myself and other mothers, my first suggestion for cultivating River Mother is to notice timing. Often, our culture urges us to move quickly—to make decisions and take action rapidly. And definitely don't look back! But our body and nervous system often tell us we need to move slower. Frequent stomach aches, headaches, or leg cramps might all be invitations to be more aware of your pace. These could be in your body, or in the body of another family member. These can be symptoms that a person is chronically fatigued or overextended.

Speed overrides the ability of the body to send subtle messages and for our awareness to receive them. This is by design. When we are forced to move at a quick pace and make decisions without careful consideration of all involved, we tend to disregard our inner sensations and default to societal expectations of how things should be. This exercise is about reclaiming your own pace.

For this activity you're going to get up and walk, so you need to have room to move. A park, yard, or large driveway can be a good place. Begin walking as fast or slow as you like. As you walk, vary your speed and direction. Change direction quickly, on a whim. Go fast. Go slow. Each time you do one of these things, pay attention to your body. Was it easy? Was it difficult? Did you resist? Did you feel happy and at ease? Look for that place of ease. What about the ways you move is easy and flowing? Does it feel like your "natural" pace? What would your easy, "natural" pace be?

Going Deeper with River Mother

Imagine that you are standing on a mountain top. You can see the river flowing downhill, meandering between the hills below, headed for the ocean. You can see the water flowing away from you, and you can see well enough to identify rapids, calm flow, and eddies along the river edges. It flows further and further, until it reaches the horizon. While you cannot see the end point of that river, you can see a long stretch of water flowing toward its destination.

Define your horizon. How far out can you see or dream for your life? It doesn't have to be the grand finale that you look toward, but maybe some significant change from where you are now. You don't have to know how to get there—that will come in time. But knowing what you're aiming for is important.

In the rush of everyday life, we often fall into a pattern of just trying to move away from what we don't want. But if we realize we're in a large and diverse landscape, moving away in a random direction will not be helpful. We need more. We need to know what we're looking for.

Allow yourself to imagine the life you really do want. Dream for a moment. The strongest dreams will be full of sensation and feeling. There can be some description of objects that you hope will be there, but there are more avenues to a feeling than to an object. Focusing on objects can lead to more constraints on the life you have, rather than making opportunities for change.

Write down your vision of your horizon. Describe the feelings and imagine the fulfilled longings. Then, bringing your attention back to right here, right now, determine the one next small step that moves in the direction of your horizon experience. It doesn't have to take you all the way, and you don't have to plan the whole journey. Simply find the next one right step.

This process is one that needs persistent fine tuning. When we use our imagination we are projecting out into the future, but we only know what we know right now. It means we must occasionally revisit our hopes and dreams and choose our "next right steps" again. It is a constantly emerging process.

FOREST MOTHER

You were never meant to do it alone.

~ Forest Mother

To be
A thread in
The "us" tapestry
~ Forest Mother

THE FOREST LANDSCAPE

Forests are made up of individual trees in groups. Trees in a forest are often connected by a deep root mat, and they cohabitate with large and small organisms to create the ecosystem. Trees, such as aspen and redwoods, communicate and share resources through their root systems. Some depend on mycelia—small organisms that facilitate sharing of nutrients among neighbors. Some trees communicate through chemical signals carried on the wind.

Interconnectedness is the hallmark of the forest system. In all ecosystems, members depend on one another, but the forest has a particularly well-developed system of communication and nutrient transfer that makes it easy to see the sharing of resources. There is an albino redwood tree in a forest near where I live. A docent once told me that it cannot photosynthesize for itself because of its lack of chlorophyll, so it cannot make its own food. The mother tree standing next to it shares her nutrients through a connected root system. The albino tree is not large, but it lives despite not being able to produce its own food.

Forests are more than just trees. Forests include the other plants and animals that live there. They are an interconnected set of organisms whose individual wellbeing feeds back into the health and resilience of the environment.

Forest ecosystems hold an immense amount of diversity and complexity with almost infinite possibilities of arrangement. They change over time and experience disruption. Certain elements may arrive or depart, but the forest remains.

Trees also store large amounts of water, affecting evaporation, precipitation, and weather. Their influence is wide-ranging and significant to other systems with which they may not be in direct contact. An example of these large-scale effects is the Amazon rainforest. Through evaporation and heat exchange, the Amazon rainforest creates weather patterns that extend for thousands of miles.

FOREST MOTHER

Forest Mother is a community mother. She is connected to other women, likes to raise her children communally, and sees the opportunity for ease in meeting each other's needs through group engagement. Forest Mother has vision, and it's big and involves everyone. She values social connection, working together, and interdependence.

Forest Mother sometimes focuses on what is above ground and beautiful, ignoring what is messier and made of microscopic workings underneath. She may turn her gaze regularly to the tops of the trees, appreciating the beauty that life has to offer. She shares her appreciation of light and breeze with others, and truly stands for living in that awareness.

When Forest Mother is deeply resourced, she will not only be attentive to the branches and the leaves, but also to the root system. She will tend to the needs and skills underlying the relationships that form the foundation of her community.

If Forest Mother is depleted, she may prioritize one value or one segment of the community over all others. She risks becoming dogmatic. Values are not hierarchical. They are messy, convoluted, and sometimes at odds. It's what makes human life as complex as it is. When we prioritize one value over all others, it negates the flexibility and potential of the situation.

Forest Mother values mutuality and consent. She holds the through line. She circles back around and checks in with others again and again. She is willing to be repetitive to make sure that everyone is taken care of as change happens. Forest Mother wants to find a way to move in which no one has to compromise their values. Life is not a zero-sum game for her. She looks for the win-win, the patterns outside of the paradigm of "if I have more then you must have less."

STRENGTHS OF FOREST MOTHER

While the value Forest Mother places on beauty (or any singular value prized above all others) is certainly valid, alone it is limiting and rigid. Human lives are lived in the between places, and our access to those places relies on our capacity for dissonance and willingness to sometimes be in tension around these feelings. It is in being able to hold both, the chaos and the beauty, that we find wholeness.

Forest Mother values cooperation and working together. She sees that alone, we are only able to do so much. But, if we do it together, we can accomplish great things. She wants to organize and coalesce people into working in parallel and sharing a common vision. Her balance is in holding both individual expectations and finding a cooperative path forward together.

She values the functional working of the family or community as a whole. Like the forest, she provides nourishment, shelter, and protection. This is due to her enormous capacity to bring together so many different perspectives. Forest Mother can unite many individuals into a diverse community with so much to offer.

This is an enormous task, and she is well aware of the complexity: the in-between, the roots, and the unseen. Beneath the forest floor is the complex web of subtle communication through mycorrhizae amid dampness, decay, and space for the water to flow through the soil. When Forest Mother expands herself enough to contain both the darkness and the sunlight at the top of the trees, to be both above and below, and to be comfortable there, that is when Forest Mother shines.

STRUGGLES OF FOREST MOTHER

Forest Mother may begin to live in the shadows under the canopy. She might fall into the darkness, the uncertainty that is in the complexity and interdependence of the forest system. She might underestimate the dangers there, or not see some of the hidden risks. She is especially prone to underestimating the trauma that makes people unpredictable. The darkness in the nooks of the forest might also be blind spots in her great vision of community.

This means that specific details, or particular relationships, may be neglected in the shadows. They can get overgrown, unkempt, covered up like the forest floor with litter. They become forgotten remnants of things that were once important. Certainly decay happens, and materials recycle through the system, but Forest Mother sometimes loses track of the details, dropping a subject before it is complete.

This "losing track" is a continuum. At the extreme, Forest Mother may collapse under the complexity of holding the forest together, falling into a dark time for herself and her work. This can also present as a lack of direct light on the tasks at hand, showing up in life as lethargy, and inattention to the roots and connections that build relationships and a sense of shared responsibility.

Ignoring the roots of the matter makes it hard for Forest Mother to change the family patterns, to choose her way directly, and to take meaningful action. She can get distracted by outer appearances, and forget that she is also on an inner journey.

Supporting community structure is not a bad thing, and we certainly need as much cooperation as we can get. But when it becomes the defining factor of our self-perception as a mother, and when others' approval of us as good mothers determines how we think of ourselves, that is the shadow of Forest Mother.

FOREST MOTHER IN PARENTING

As a healthy parent, Forest Mother is a good protector and provider. She provides her children abundant food and shelter with opportunities for exploration and play. Because she values and nurtures her community, there are likely plenty of other children around to play with, and lots of adults to guide and protect. The resources of the community are shared, and children can trust many adults to help them if they require assistance. Opportunities for exploration, learning, and understanding would be available to all of the children through all of the adults.

However, Forest Mother is also susceptible to the influence of cultural messages about how she *should* appear as a mother, how she *should* function so as to be seen as a "Good Mother." If she forgets to set her own North Star as her guide, she might begin to say yes to volunteering not because it's where she wants to put her energy, but because she thinks she needs to please others, or it makes her feel worthy of being part of the group. One common example of this is the overcommitted mom. She shows up to every opportunity to support the community systems, at the expense of her family. Her need to be needed and to be seen as a good mother override her needs for connection with her family.

While I always appreciate the parents willing to spend their time on these tasks, and I know that many organizations would crumble without the work of volunteers, I also know that the pressure to say yes to these things is enormous.

In case this feels like it's hitting close to home, this is a good place to remember that one of the pillars of Landscape of Mothers is that these struggles are not bad or good in isolation. Everything depends on the context, the needs of the group, and the needs of the individuals within the group. Forest Mother's task is to find her own ways through tending to the inner workings of her family, as well as showing up and sharing her gifts in her community.

It's really compelling to do mothering in the public sphere. Often, that's the only place we get gratitude for doing so much support work. I certainly didn't feel like my family understood the work it took to run the house, plan and cook the meals, and get everyone to their events. If this physical, mental, and emotional labor begins to weigh on us, such that we feel invisible, unsupported, or unappreciated, we might turn to doing work in a more public way through which we feel more rewarded.

THE INNATE GIFT OF FOREST MOTHER

The central gift of Forest Mother is belonging. She navigates the relationship between intimacy and independence. Our culture tends to over-value individualism, do-it-yourself attitudes, and pulling yourself up by your bootstraps, which can lead to the isolation that Island and Desert Mothers grapple with.

Forest Mother wants more than anything to belong. She wants to be accepted into the larger group. She desires interconnection and interdependence. Honestly, human physiology is on her side. We are inherently wired to be together, to function as a group, and to find safety in connection. Babies find comfort in being held and cared for, and they fail to thrive without enough attention and interaction with others. It's in our very nature.

However, social pressure to conform often replaces true belonging. It is conditional, revocable, and dependent on what others want from us more than what's best for our own well-being. This is a tough dance, because common understandings and agreements form the foundation of community. In communities that are not good at communication, shared understandings often turn into requirements of admission for the group. These situations encourage us to sacrifice our uniqueness, our individual truth, for group membership. While that can feel like belonging at first, it always takes a toll and can become internal fracturing of the Self for survival.

When we conform in order to be accepted, we are engaging in a form of self-abandonment. We are ourselves rejecting parts of us that have been rejected by our social group. To do this, we have to push back and contain some part of us that is expressing something unwanted in the collective. Or something we don't know how to grapple with. Anytime we "suck it up" and put on a happy face so we can be in a group, anytime we feel like we have to hide how we really feel, we are choosing conformity over belonging.

Forest Mother really shines in our lives when we stop bouncing back and forth between isolation and immersion, and we begin to integrate time and tasks for both. Our nervous systems thrive on having *both* connection *and* solitude. We do not have to choose one over the other.

CULTIVATING FOREST MOTHER

Somatic practices can help us transform our internal gifts to external expression. We relate with each other and the Mothers through sensation and experience. The following activities are suggestions for how you might connect with Forest Mother through your body in addition to reading about her.

> *The Forest Mother Question: What would it be like to be in this life together in ways that serve all involved?*

Forest Mother Activity

Forest Mother's primary gift is belonging, through honoring both her need for social relationships and her internal need to tend to herself. Going even deeper than finding balance, she integrates community and self.

Give yourself a few minutes with a piece of paper and a pen, plus something that feels focusing and soothing (tea, candle, scent, or cozy blanket... whatever lets you settle into yourself easily and comfortably).

Make two columns. Label one "Together" and the other "By Myself." While connection is positive, our well-being comes from having some time together with others, and some time to ourselves. Separate your tasks for the day or the week into the two columns. Which do you want to do with someone else, and which do you want to do alone?

Do these two columns feel like they meet your needs? Do you have as much connective and together time as would feel nourishing to you? Do you have enough time to yourself?

For future days or weeks, how would you like to rebalance these? Note that these are not static needs. They shift as the context shifts. It is okay for these lists and needs to morph over time alongside the current state of the household. Adjust as necessary.

Going Deeper with Forest Mother

This activity requires the ability to have your hands on some natural objects such as rocks, sticks, leaves, or shells. You can do this indoors, though I highly recommend doing it outside if you can.

This nature practice puts us in touch with the world around us. It makes space for us to notice that we are interacting with an environment, a context larger than us, and that we belong in it as one part of a whole.

The invitation is to take your objects and create some arrangement that feels good to your system. It doesn't have to make sense or look beautiful. Follow your own desire about where to put your objects and how to group them. Let the arrangement arise from within you. Notice the objects. They will have unique characteristics and shared ones. Allow the pieces of nature that you are working with relate to each other as you place them. Work with what you have until it feels complete.

When the arrangement feels complete, spend a couple of minutes contemplating it. What do you like about it? What do you not like? What themes are there between objects or the way you placed them? Does it relate to anything that is front-and-center in your life right now?

This can be a very simple project that takes a few minutes, or an elaborate one that takes hours. One is not better than the other. You also don't have to know if it means anything. It's okay if you look at it and aren't sure if there's anything that connects it to your life. The act of making art with natural objects and your presence and action is enough. The contact with nature is soothing to the nervous system, and your interaction with nature through art is an act of relationship.

OCEAN MOTHER

May your oceanic heart change the human tide

~ Ocean Mother

Who breathes
Me to life?
My good ancestors
~ Ocean Mother

THE OCEAN LANDSCAPE

The ocean contains multitudes. It is deep and shallow, quick and imperceptibly slow. It is tumultuous and dreamy. Life began in the ocean, and the fluids of our bodies mimic those salty, watery conditions. The ocean is a source of not only life, but of the very conditions for life. Without the ocean our planet would not be as it is. The vast quantities of water in the ocean keep our temperatures mild, our lands hydrated, and our rivers flowing.

Whatever is going on at the surface of the ocean, the waves and storms and moods, it also contains depths full of generative stillness that underpin it all. It contains secrets and a vastness we usually associate with the heavens. The ocean is the container for so much more than we know.

There's also a connection between the vast pool of creation water and our consciousness. The ocean contains things we would never have guessed, like the strange creatures living at the bottom of the sea. What is in the deep is mostly unknown. We actually know more about distant space than we do about the ocean depths. And yet, it also contains the shallows, the "nursery" of life. The warm, salty, fluids that gave rise to life. The shallow waters, where humans and so many other species, flock to the beaches and harbors for rest and relaxation.

OCEAN MOTHER

Ocean Mother is deep and reflective. She considers things slowly and carefully, churning them over within her until she feels certain. She is thoughtful, thorough, and rhythmic. You can count on her careful consideration.

She is the salty fluid from which life began, so she is our source, and as such, holds our earliest experiences. In fact, she really holds us in our entirety, as she grew us and nourished us in her womb. Our consciousness still finds itself in Ocean Mother—we are eternally connected to her.

Ocean Mother holds the joys and the deep wounds of our childhood. We may think we already dealt with the old wounds, and maybe we mostly did, but Ocean Mother will resurface any that are unhealed. It's very common for the stress or trauma you experienced, to come up again as anxiety or fear when your child is that same age. Old wounds can also arise amidst a crisis with one of your parents, which often brings up the feelings around childhood pains.

For better or worse, our emotional lives are connected to Ocean Mother and the watery depths, where secrets, trauma, guilt, shame, and anger reside. The opportunity is to explore deeply, extensively, and sometimes in the dark. Ocean Mother offers us the possibility of embracing it all. We cannot change our history, but we can learn to be in relationship with it differently. Ocean Mother is our ally in re-membering ourselves. She helps us relocate our wholeness, and cultivate compassion and empathy.

At her best, Ocean Mother is calm, peaceful, and aware. She goes with the flow most of the time, though she likes things to be regular and consistent. Her pace is fairly slow. She is thoughtful and tends to be conscious of her impact.

She is likely to be the kind of person who accumulates books or information about what she values most deeply.

STRENGTHS OF OCEAN MOTHER

The strengths of Ocean Mother are many. You could say she is our consciousness or awareness. Like Island Mother and Mountain Mother, Ocean Mother has a gift for listening. Ocean Mother beckons for us to listen to our spiritual connections. She invites us to know not only ourselves, but the greater experience of life force energy that holds us.

Spiritual practice underlies the strengths of Ocean Mother. She is dedicated to her inner growth and awareness. She feels a deep connection to Earth and to life force energy. Her house is probably filled with trinkets from nature, like acorns, feathers, leaves, sticks and rocks. If not nature material, then there are probably shrines of figures and artifacts that are meaningful to her in her home. These serve as intentional focal points for connection with the rhythms of life and death.

Spirituality arises from her relationship with all of the Mothers. Ocean Mother weaves together trust, self-definition, solitude, presence, purpose, and connection. She holds the exploration of the Mothers as a spiritual practice—the practice of settling into trust and presence, and seeing reflected the best of ourselves. We don't cultivate this mirror of the best of ourselves to bypass the things that need work. Instead, we see our strengths honestly and humbly and learn to use them for building the world in which we want to live.

Details are important to Ocean Mother. Each part of her life has meaning and purpose that needs to be tended and sustained. She is a delicate balance of harmonies. Her spiritual practice, whatever that might look like, is a big part of what helps Ocean Mother stay healthy. It may be related to the Earth, and it is grounded in detail and a sense of right relationship with her environment.

She gathers many details about the things that are important to her, and as much as she likes to know the facts, she's also willing to follow her instinct or intuition on how to get there. She doesn't prioritize her head over her heart or gut as an information source.

Ocean Mother knows the value of embodied knowledge as her internal guidance system. She carries the capacity to be with the unknown. Her sense of sacred connection and interdependence creates a resilience we cannot get from guarding or protecting. Ocean Mother stands for being with what is.

She invites us to always be present to the process of knowing ourselves. She encourages us to move slowly in figuring that out, and to dive deep when appropriate. She asks us to consider what kind of life we want to have. And maybe most importantly, she reminds us that we are held by something bigger than us that is always present. We may call it God, or we might call it Spirit, or maybe Life Force Energy. Whatever that life-affirming energy of all connected living things is, whatever we call it, Ocean Mother invites us to remember it.

STRUGGLES OF OCEAN MOTHER

Because Ocean Mother holds our wounds, she may also hold any guilt or shame we may have about motherhood. There are almost infinite types of guilt and shame, such as fertility in the face of others' infertility, a previous pregnancy that was aborted or miscarried, how we feel about our parents, or how we are behaving as mothers. We might also carry guilt about what we perceive we are giving to our children, or not giving them. There might be uncertainty around our own skills as a mother.

Are we good enough mothers?

Ocean Mother can also experience overwhelm. Because she sees such a big picture, she has collected the details, and she wants so much to be a Good Mother, she can end up pulled in too many directions and insufficiently committed to any single one. She can also become bogged down in the "too muchness" of the responsibilities involved in parenting.

As an extension of her overwhelm, she might feel very needy. Ocean Mother has a lot going on internally. She may often want to be soothed by others. She may struggle to acknowledge when she needs help. And asking for help may trigger her shame around not being able to do it all herself. This may also cause her to have a lot of intense feelings around the needs and demands of her children.

If she externalizes this shame, she may use blaming and shaming tactics on her children in order to motivate them. This can backfire, as it feels bad to be shamed into doing something, even if it is something necessary or beneficial. And so the child's resistance to being blamed and shamed leads to a lack of compliance that feeds overwhelm and uncertainty in the parent.

I felt this way a lot when my children were small and needed a lot of my attention. It turned out that I also needed a lot of my attention. I felt torn between being needed by my kids and a sense of shame that my own neediness arose simultaneously. It felt like I could either tend to me or to them, but not both. I was in a double bind that made mothering harder than it needed to be. Tapping into Sun and Moon Mother's gift of focusing on self-regulation and Mountain Mother's tending practices helped a great deal.

OCEAN MOTHER IN PARENTING

Ocean Mother understands mothering to be a very complex, deep, and intricately involved process. She sees the bigness of it—it's not just what she does with her own children, but how she influences the perspectives of her children, how that ripples into the community, and how those ripples shape the future. This may cause trouble in being able to apply all of her theory and understanding into tangible action in the here and now. It overwhelms Ocean Mother that she can't possibly know enough to "get it right," and this keeps her from being in the moment.

Ocean Mother has emotional intelligence skills, relationship skills, and communication skills. If she doesn't have those tools she does what needs to be done to acquire them. Her children's health and wellbeing is her goal. She sees the big picture of their growth and has her eye on a diverse definition of their happiness as adults. It's not just about a single measure of success. She wants her children to be well-rounded and happy with good relationships.

Occasionally she will get stirred up into an angry storm, but she is present enough to take responsibility pretty quickly. Ocean Mother recognizes the effect she has on her children and will apologize easily when it is warranted. She is mindful, cognizant, and aware of her impact on her children. She sees how certain things she says or does will send an unspoken message. She's as careful about what is unsaid as she is about her spoken words.

Internalized blame and shame from childhood will often become part of Ocean Mother's internal dialogue. Our inner mechanisms of self-control are built on the ways that other people influenced our behavior. As we develop self-control, if it's modeled on shame and blame to get conformity, we develop a strong inner voice that also uses shame and blame toward ourselves. The risk in parenting is that shame becomes the default setting to get our children to do what we want or need them to do.

Ocean Mother not only *knows* the enormity of motherhood ... she *contains* every bit of it. The worry, grief, anticipation, joy, surrender, and loving focus of mothering is all inside of Ocean Mother. She can feel all of these things at once. She supports the awareness of the complexity of what motherhood means. Ocean Mother encompasses the full range of emotion of the incredible upheaval it is to bring a new baby into your home.

Between the hormones, lifestyle changes, sacrifices, and expectations of being a new mother, it is almost certain not to be the idyllic story we dreamed it would be. The best part of Ocean Mother is that she also contains the invitation to float—to feel buoyant and supported as we surrender to being held by something bigger than ourselves.

THE INNATE GIFT OF OCEAN MOTHER

The innate gift of Ocean Mother is spirituality. This is a big topic, and I want to clarify what I mean by it. In the context of the *Landscape of Mothers*, spirituality has three components. First, it is something bigger than us that is always present and never absent. Second, spirituality is mindfulness that links us to our sense of deeper meaning. Last, it invokes a sense of awe and gratitude that we can act on.

Ocean Mother is bigger than us. She represents all that we cannot see. She holds the recognition that we are a part of the Universe—we are embedded in this time and place. She reminds us that we are in the presence of a larger and more complex system of life.

However you already refer to this element in your life is perfect. I don't have a prescription for what you should call it or what you should believe about it. I am more interested in whether or not you have practices for relating to this "bigger than you" part of life. We can practice simply noticing what we are held in and what forces we participate with to create life. At their root, spiritual practices are all forms of sitting with the unknown.

Within Landscape of Mothers, there is a natural expression of spirituality as connection with nature, with something more enduring than us. Something larger and longer. It is more than the human world. Nature expresses a comprehensive array of ways that we can be in relationship with others, and we can go to nature with the clear intent to reflect and learn.

Second, Ocean Mother fosters a sense of meaningfulness that can be expressed through consciously noticing and being aware within our everyday lives. The context of being embedded in a spiritual world allows us to see the details and effects of our actions differently. These awarenesses are a foundation of the capacity to listen deeply, bring awareness to the surface, and honor meaning. Actions and behaviors based on this foundation of spirituality are the rituals that hold us and settle us.

Last, our spirituality invokes a sense of awe and gratitude at the enormity, diversity, and delicacy of it all. Following our spirituality affords us opportunities to find great joy in and celebrate what is most meaningful to us. We can appreciate and communicate that appreciation for all that is miraculous.

Ocean Mother beckons us back to her, to return to her wisdom through ourselves. After all, we are mostly water. The invitation is to return to her through remembering our own center. She asks us to come and float—let her hold us in her womb-like embrace as we surrender to the buoyancy of her waters. When we surrender and allow ourselves to be held, we can listen deeply.

Listening to our bodies, our emotions, our thoughts, and our hearts is a radical act. Mostly we are taught to control our inner world, not invite it to talk to us. We are taught to make sure others get what they want or need. We are taught who is most important and worthy of attention, and it is never ourselves. To be the object of our own attention is one of the steps in our own healing. It is the beginning of putting our bones back together... It is the re-membering.

Maybe it all comes down to meaning. I have spoken many prayers to and for my younger selves who have been through so much and survived. I want to be deeply aware of meaning in my own life, and discerning about what meaning is mine. I believe the emotional body has something for me there. Emotions are how we know what is, in fact, our meaning to grapple with. Meaning depends on what we know and what we're willing to see. This can change over time.

What if we lived lives of meaningfulness instead of mindfulness? Or mindfulness followed by meaningfulness? Mindfulness is something I can bring to any moment. I can notice and be aware; I can feel and listen. Sometimes meaningfulness arises within that context... but sometimes it doesn't. There are tasks I have to do that I just do not like. They do not hold fulfillment or enjoyment for me. They are simply there.

And then there are the tasks where I do find meaning. I can be mindful and present with them, and in return I feel filled up and nourished. Meaningfulness feels like it orients toward the things that are important to me, toward my values and my fulfillment.

Undoubtedly we do both every day. Being present is one part (Mountain Mother's part), and meaningfulness is another (Ocean Mother's part). Ocean Mother orients us toward living full lives with depth, laughter, consistency, and change. Meaning is one way Ocean Mother invites us to navigate.

CULTIVATING OCEAN MOTHER

Body-centered spiritual practices bring the intangible to our lives. Through our bodies we are able to express in action what it is that we believe. The following activities are suggestions for how you might get to know Ocean Mother and see how she shows up in your life.

The Ocean Mother Question: What holds me?

Ocean Mother Activity

You can do this practice at any time. You can sit, stand, or lay down. The purpose is to create a pause, particularly when you are hearing a lot of your inner critic. Sometimes it helps to practice this when you are not in an active dialogue with the inner critic, so that the practice is easy to recall in a more critical moment.

The practice of Ocean Mother is to pause. Put your hand on your heart and belly, and wish yourself some wellness, happiness, and ease. This interrupts any of the critical internal thoughts that want to motivate through shame and blame. It also gives a little room for comfort, for you being held by something bigger. It creates space to listen to your internal guidance. This is an act of unconditional positive regard for the self. It is showing yourself respect, openness, the benefit of the doubt. You are allowing yourself to be as you are, and to take your next right step from there.

Personally, I call this a prayer because it changes something in me. You might call it something else. This is a bit different than a similar exercise we did with Wind Mother that was focused on trusting our own breath. With Ocean Mother we are fostering thoughts of protection and nurturing toward ourselves. We're learning to mother ourselves well. We're giving our inner child those messages we may not have received as children, now that we are "the adult in the room."

Going Deeper with Ocean Mother

I invite you to write this one out. Gather paper, a favorite writing instrument, and a timer (a phone will do if you silence notifications for the duration of the activity). Find someplace you won't be interrupted. You can set your timer for 5 minutes or 15 minutes or anything in between. In this case, longer is usually better.

> *At the top of the page write:*
> **What is bigger than me that holds me and makes me feel better?**

> *On the rest of the page, answer this question as many times as you can in the time allotted. Keep answering the same single question over and over. The thing is, there is often no one simple, concise answer. There are many answers, many versions of the answer... from very tangible things to thoughts to faith to curiosity. The answers may be extremely varied, and letting ourselves answer more than once or a few times gives us a chance to get deeper into the answer. We get to move closer to our unconscious, to the things we haven't thought of before. So, just keep writing. Try not to think too hard. Write down*

the ridiculous and the perplexing. Let them all be there. You can edit later for things that make sense. In the writing phase, just allow whatever arises.

This writing exercise is about getting in touch with our spiritual center. It is putting words to what we feel holds us even when we can't see anything at all.

It's a bit like when we look up at the stars at night, and the bigness of it all reminds us of how small we are. We are part of a much bigger universe. Or it is like floating in the water and feeling held in safety and surrender, as if in a womb. Ocean Mother can do that for us. She returns us to ourselves. She returns us to the rhythm of our heartbeat, to the flow of our breath, to our body.

PART II: Working with Landscape of Mothers

LANDSCAPES AND OUR INNER ECOLOGY

Landscape of Mothers is anchored in the movement, cycles, and interconnectedness of the natural world. When we interact with the more-than-human world, we become aware and learn ways of being that we can apply to our human relationships.

We can envision nature as a container. It is our environment and our context. Whatever happens is embedded inside of the natural world. For most of us, this is bigger than our usual task-focused human-centric view. Noticing nature as a container offers us the gifts of spaciousness and new perspective. With these gifts in hand, we can intentionally seek out natural elements that make us feel calmer and healthier, and give us a sense of belonging.

Ecotherapy—the use of nature to address stress and tension in the body and mind—is becoming quite widespread and popular. Scientific study of the human response to nature has shown benefits such as lower blood pressure, better sleep, and mood improvement. I'm happy to have the science there, but to me, the most important effect is that time outside in nature helps me feel connected to something nourishing. It just feels good in my body.

Being aware of and in relationship to the natural world gives us context, a place to begin, good ground from which to take action. The "ecology of us" is embedded in the "ecology of place" that we inhabit. We are not separate from the world; we are woven into it. This means that we are never alone, life force energy is always present, and we are in community with nature.

Natural systems have solved a great number of survival and relationship problems. Many different organisms have adapted and figured out how to coexist in a forest, for example. We only have to allow ourselves to be held by nature, and to listen, in order to begin to see the application to our own lives. The steps the natural world has taken to solve problems can be a good starting place when we don't know what to do.

When it feels like so much is happening internally that inquiry into our own bodies creates more anxiety, it's a good time to connect with nature. Earth can serve as the wise elder, the one who holds, the one who comforts and strengthens.

Seeking nature as a guide isn't meant to be a one-time activity. You absolutely can go out in nature with a question and receive some awareness that moves you. But, in my experience, it's meant to be a relationship we continually develop. A relationship like any other, which shifts and changes and is ongoing. Frequency of visits, intensity of interaction, and duration are all flexible. Consider what kinds of interactions support your human relationships. What is it that you most appreciate and feel supported by in terms of their frequency, intensity, and duration? When we bring that level of commitment to the natural world, we are most likely to receive powerful reflection in return.

Natural systems can be a safe place to work out some of the difficulties we have with other humans. Our relationship with nature begins with nervous system regulation. When we are well-regulated, our bodies experience a calming effect—a sense of solidity and reliability that we sometimes lack in challenging relationships.

Settling in with nature can bring a felt sense of safety.

With nature we don't have to be good, or right, or smart. We can show up as we are. We don't have to "get with the program" or worry about what nature thinks of us. The unconditional presence of nature, no matter who you are, is a healing aspect. It calls us to notice the spaciousness in our outer and inner environments, and lets us be who we are. We don't have an obligation to nature to respond. We can just be with ourselves in the moment.

Nature is neutral about what we should do. It has no advice, no judgment. So, when we go to nature and we find regulation, what is in us that needs to be known can arise. What is in our subconscious can draw our attention to a mirror in nature. Following what catches our interest, trusting our body and nature to align, we may find a new perspective or solution to our difficulty.

Landscape of Mothers is a map to navigating these relationships with the natural world, and then, by extension, with our human family. We can use the understanding of our own positions and motivations that we gain in our work with the ecology of place to help us navigate the meaningful relationships in our lives. The Mothers hold us as we receive guidance, awareness, and perspective that we may not have seen through our learned, habitual, or human relationship lenses. We can trust in nature—trust that it holds us and whatever we're struggling with, nature has already devised a solution.

Walking with Landscape Mothers is a time for remembering and making space for the whole of who we are. We dedicate ourselves to openness and being true to ourselves. It doesn't matter if it's about parenting, or work, or friendships, or community. This path is a personal practice of showing up fully and honestly to our everyday lives. It is available, not only to mothers, but to anyone who values a culture of care and togetherness.

FEAR OR DISTRUST OF NATURE

The invitation of Landscape of Mothers to build a relationship with nature need not push you to do something that feels beyond your capability or capacity in any way. There are so many ways to be in touch with nature.

Fear of nature, or maybe not something even that strong—a distrust, perhaps, or distaste for being outdoors—doesn't need to keep you from working with Landscape of Mothers. There are ways of engaging nature in your imagination, in parks, and in cultivated natural areas. I encourage you to engage with the natural world in whatever context allows you to be comfortable while still exposing you to something new. That something new can be in the environment, or it can be in your own self.

One note about the fear of natural systems. Our brains are wired to look for threats to our survival, and one of the biggest threats comes from what we do not know or understand. Many people have fears of things lurking in the woods, fears of being far away from help should we need it, and general fear of the wild and wilderness (what we cannot know or predict). Some of this comes from popular media, survivalist shows, and horror movies in which isolation and the inability to get help is part of the way characters get into trouble.

This is the edge we learn from. When we feel safe, we easily soothe ourselves and regulate our own nervous system. We are open to new thoughts, ideas, and sensations. If our bodies feel exposed and unprotected, the stress mechanisms of our nervous system turn on, and the associated hormones inhibit learning, openness, and relaxation. So, don't feel that you have to go to the extreme to engage with this work. Don't push yourself faster, harder, or further than where you feel safe. In this case, going slower will actually get you there faster.

ENGAGING WITH NATURE

To engage with nature, our first thought is often to go outside. That works if you have some of these landscapes in your local environment and they are accessible. That is by no means the only way. The landscapes in this book may only be in your area in small ways. Sitting with a rock may be the access you have to a mountain. A creek through the city may be the "river" you know. Engagement begins with noticing the characteristics of the landscape that you can be in contact with, no matter how small.

If certain landscapes presented in this book are not accessible to you for any reason, because of physical proximity, ability to travel, fears or distaste, time, or just because you don't feel like going out today, you can utilize other methods of connecting with landscape. One method is simply imagining the landscape you wish to explore. What do you already know about or associate with that landscape? You can also visit the Landscape of Mothers Pinterest boards at https://www.landscapeofmothers.com/lom-image-board.html, where you can look at images that reflect the physical landscape itself, life forms that live there, or the intangible qualities associated with the landscape. If you are a visual person, this is a really helpful resource.

Once you've decided how to approach nature—through your imagination, photos, or by going on location—your practice there is threefold. Notice, remain neutral, and learn from your encounter.

Notice. Be honest with yourself about your comfort with nature. Once you get there, it's time to be observant and notice. I promise that you don't have to be out in the wilderness. I've had revelations from the natural world by just taking out the trash. Granted, usually it tends to happen more easily when I am intentional, but I have had spontaneous encounters that left a long and deep impression about how I live my life. I know others who have had that quick and unexpected wisdom experience, too.

Neutrality. When we approach anything with preconceived notions, we tend to miss what else is there that we didn't expect. It's fine for us to have expectations and hopes. But when we can allow nature to show us what is true for the landscape, an animal, or a plant, we have the opportunity to learn something new about ourselves. We don't have to agree with what we see in nature. There is no requirement to adopt the solution nature offers. The invitation is to stand in a neutral place, so we can see something new or inspiring to us that we might not have noticed otherwise.

Learn. When we see something in the natural world that resonates within us, it's important to do the learning. That is, to take the wisdom into our lives and utilize it in some meaningful way. Allow it to transform our behaviors, and shift our thought patterns, and integrate it with what we already know. This takes some attention and awareness, as our brains are wired to verify what we already believe, regardless of whether those beliefs are correct. True learning involves taking in new information and being willing to address its conflicts with what we already hold as true. Learning is the invitation to take action based on our new knowledge or perspective.

This is a repetitive practice, a way of being with nature that supports our internal growth and development. It's a practice of reclaiming ourselves from the damage that other humans have (intentionally or unintentionally) caused in our minds, our psyches, and our nervous systems. There is little structure to the process. There is no timeline or set up or "right way." That's why I call it a practice. It's a new perspective on life so that our guidance can come from (or be validated for us by) Mother Nature.

Nature does this in ordinary ways that I don't think humans always appreciate. The plants that grow through the cracks in the concrete are somehow finding a way to grow in places made inhospitable. Whole civilizations have been absorbed into the water, sand, soil, and plant life on the planet. It is the great resilience of nature that helps us keep going when life feels hardest.

A FEW WORDS
ON ARCHETYPES

An archetype is a representative and recurring symbol in dialogue, literature, or entertainment that reflects a universal pattern in human nature. Archetypes are symbols, characters, or places that exhibit characteristics that are common among large groups of people. In Jungian psychology, archetypes are seen as representatives of shared experiences in the collective unconscious.

The Mother archetypes help us locate ourselves in the vast array of what it is to be human. In this practice, the mother archetypes act as a system of partitioning the wholeness of being human into manageable parts so that we can think in detail about something that's difficult, or impossible, to grasp all at once.

The benefit of exploring with archetypes is that we avoid "biting off more than we can chew." We take a smaller chunk and truly consider what we have. This perspective shift may feel significant and impactful. We can better integrate new realizations into our whole perspective and find increased understanding, compassion, and clarity. We are more aware of our own capacities and we can use them with intention and awareness.

Nature archetypes are especially powerful because nature is universally understood at some level. The archetypes are also specific enough to clearly have certain characteristics and not others. That means that they are subsets of wholeness. And within those subsets, archetypes of nature are consistent, and yet also changeable enough, to have understandable patterns to them. This makes room for our unique way of being in the world to be reflected back at us.

Each *Landscape of Mothers* archetype embodies gifts and skills for us to explore. With this practice and exploration, these skills become more present and integrated in a lived experience kind of way, and they are easily accessible when we need them. That is, we practice in our everyday lives so that we can access the core gifts of the Mothers when we are struggling or in crisis.

And so, let us begin our journey!

LANDSCAPE OF MOTHERS
AS A NATURE PRACTICE

We have talked about what it means to work with nature and how archetypes assist us in that exploration. Now we will place those ideas in the Landscape of Mothers process. We can literally take *any* question to nature, but Landscape of Mothers offers us a container or context for doing that work.

As we approach nature, the archetype we choose to work with gives us a lens through which we formulate questions. The Landscape Mothers helps interpret what we see in nature. She is the framework for turning guidance into our next step.

CHOOSING A LANDSCAPE MOTHER

Intuitive Choice
Pick one, any one. Ultimately they are all connected. We can see their interconnectedness because each Mother shares some aspects with her neighbors. Using intuition to choose one can make room for your subconscious to make a choice that might surprise you.

Relative to a current experience
You can choose to work with a particular Mother because something is coming up in your life that you can see in one of the Mothers. It

might be her strength or her struggle. You might recognize something you resonate with in what she stands for or her behaviors. Exploring her other characteristics can give clues to a resolution or next right step.

Let yourself be chosen
Sometimes a Mother chooses us in meditation or intentional journey work. We can simply ask for an appropriate Landscape or Mother to meet us in a realm of altered awareness so that we can access unknown or unexplored content from our own psyche. This gives us the chance to let ourselves move through the Landscape from a place of curiosity that is less driven by our cognitive mind.

After choosing a Mother to work with, you might know exactly what it is that she represents for you, and exactly the struggle or celebration you are in, at this moment. If not, consider what she is coming forward with to assist you. I boil my process down to four different parts.

FOUR PHASES OF JOURNEY

Keep in mind that sometimes the characteristics or perspectives of the Mother that goes with us is as significant as the place we go. You don't have to go to the mountains with Mountain Mother. You can take Mountain Mother to the river landscape and you can still look for stability in flow, for example. Any Mother can join you in the exploration of any landscape and can be present to any part of the journey.

Also, for any one inquiry, we may go to nature multiple times in order to walk through the whole process. If desired, we can choose to take our inquiry to another Mother or landscape. If we stop after a single inquiry, we may only have a limited awareness of our situation. To grow, or shift what is bothering you, the awareness generated has to be complete enough to get pulled through to taking action. As you get answers, more questions may arise, and you can continue to go to nature until you have what you need.

The four phases of utilizing Landscape of Mothers are inquiry, noticing, guidance, and reflection. In the inquiry phase we are putting the question into words.

Inquiry

Once you've chosen a Mother to work with, it's time to figure out what question you want to take to her. This is probably the hardest step. It's where we bump into trying to control the process and outcome. The desire to "get something important" tries to come in and organize the question. It's also where we may even want to use this work to validate something we're already feeling strongly about.

The more you can let this be an intuitive, emerging process, the more you'll probably get from it. You can go in with a topic that you want to make room to contemplate, or you can define a question ahead of time. If you feel stuck, you can pick a situation that you are struggling with, choose a Landscape Mother, and simply take the question: "What would nature do in this situation?"

Example Inquiry 1: I was struggling with a time of change, wondering what my role was in my family and my community. I took the question "What do I need to let go in order to move forward?" into the forest. Belonging and relationship with others is the realm of the Forest Mother, and so it felt like the right place to look for guidance. That day I understood some very fundamental aspects of my life that needed re-examination.

Example Inquiry 2: There was a time I was stretched thin emotionally, mentally, and physically. I was headed out on vacation where I would be near the ocean, and so I took the question "How do you rest?" to Ocean Mother. I chose her to ask because I was already going to be near the water. It was convenient and practical. Asking the question over and over with Ocean Mother gave me many responses that I could implement in different parts of my life.

Noticing

When we have our question and we go to nature with it, we will have some experience. We may not always recognize that experience, but even "nothing" coming to grab our attention can be something. This takes practice. It is the act of noticing what draws your attention, what interests you. When we let our subconscious scan the environment, we can trust it to land on something meaningful.

Example Noticing 1: In the early days of my nature practice, before the Landscape of Mothers, I would go into nature and just notice what I noticed. One day I sat down, took a few breaths, and waited. Literally nothing drew my attention. So, I started looking for things. No bugs to watch, no flowers to contemplate... nothing. There wasn't even a breeze. And then I realized that "nothing" was what I needed to notice. I realized how exhausted I was, how overwhelmed, and how much I longed for rest.

Example Noticing 2: Without an inquiry, I took the garbage from my kitchen to the outdoor can. Between a plant pot and the wall of the garage was a spider weaving a web. It was breezy outside, and when her incomplete web waved precariously in the wind, she would stop weaving, and just hold on. When the breeze died down, she resumed her work. A really strong thought arose: "I want to hold my life like that." I realized that I wanted to ride the inevitable waves of life holding onto the things that were important; to fight less, and to come out of the turbulence still building, weaving, and creating. I understood how much that meant to me in that moment, and it has stuck with me for many years.

Guidance

Guidance is the desire to move in a particular direction based on the awareness that arises from the original inquiry and the noticing. This phase is an invitation to take action on our own behalf. It could be a goal, embracing a way of being, or even taking a break. The guidance indicates the next right step according to our internal systems. It's the interpretation of what you noticed.

Example Guidance 1: In a time of grief I went to a tree in my backyard. I committed to asking the tree over and over how to hold heartbreak. For the first few days I leaned on the tree and felt soothed. About a week in, I sat back a bit and noticed how close this tree was to its neighbor. It felt like a big noticing moment. I felt the "aha" feeling that arises when something meaningful catches my attention. I felt it was really important that the trees were so close. I imagined that their roots intertwined underground, and saw their canopies touching like they were holding hands above me. I needed to learn how to hold heartbreak together, rather than sitting in it by myself.

Example Guidance 2: A client was struggling to feel settled. Her attempts to soothe herself through focusing on her body were not working. We chose an external resource, a tree outside her house. We mimicked the tree's movements, swaying and slowing down to the pace of nature. She grew aware of the settling in her body, calling in the power of Mountain Mother. Once that sensation arrived she realized that her grounding was in her feet. Her guidance was to keep up the practice of dancing with the trees and cultivating the sense of strength and presence at her feet. She did this for a few days in a row, and found herself taking a stand for her needs in a new way.

Reflection

Reflection happens after everything else. It is the time where we assess what we learned that feels correct in our system. We check that the guidance feels appropriate for the present context of our lives. That is, we need to consider the impact on others who depend on us. It may take time and additional energy to figure out how to get what we need while making sure that we are not causing harm in doing it. Reflection is the step in which we integrate our intuitive guidance with our logical thought processes to figure out how we are going to do what is needed.

The Landscape of Mothers process and visits to nature can allow us to see the effects and outcomes of the patterns we're playing out in our lives. This is often easier to perceive in nature than when it is entwined with personal dynamics between complex humans. This is when nature's ability to be neutral can be really helpful. This can also uncover a subsequent layer of inquiry, either clarifying and refining your original inquiry, or by raising the next question.

Example Reflection: In Example Inquiry 1, I told a story of taking a question to Forest Mother: "What do I need to let go in order to move forward?" I got several answers that day, but one was to let go of everything I thought was foundational to my life. This required some discernment. I felt very clearly that something I thought would be important going forward, wouldn't. But, I also didn't feel that my guidance was to blow up my entire life and make everything new either. It took reflection and discernment as I went through the things I assumed I would continue to build on. It was my work. It was changing. About a month later, I was going to bed one night, and

I had the thought "Landscape of Mothers." It caught my attention. I knew it was a title. I wrote it down. And that night I wrote, turned my light off to sleep, turned it back on, wrote more, and so on. Eventually I started writing by moonlight. Wind Mother presented herself to me that night, and we began writing this book.

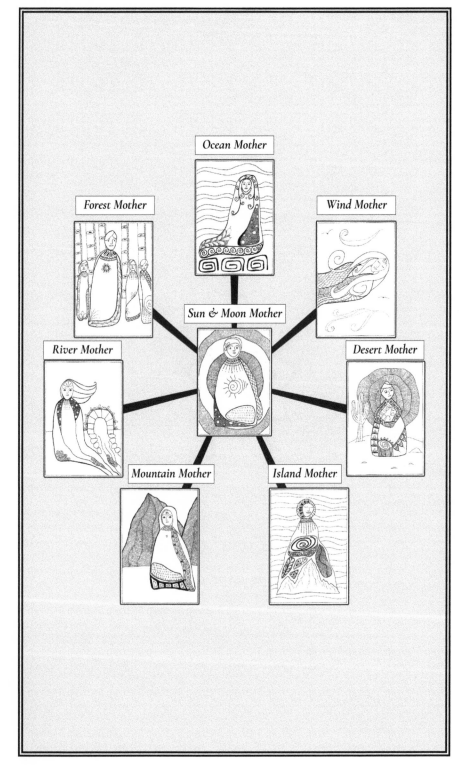

LANDSCAPE OF MOTHERS
AS A WHEEL

The archetypes in Landscape of Mothers can be approached as a wheel. Each Mother shares some common ground with her neighbors. The Mothers naturally flow from one to another. I recommend beginning with Sun and Moon Mother. Working your way around the circle, you will become familiar with each Mother's strengths and struggles in turn.

DEFINITION OF THE WHEEL

As the Landscape Mothers were becoming clearer to me, I laid them out in a circle or a wheel. It felt right because I could see their interdependence and how they interact with one another. The wheel made it feel like I could move from one to another repeatedly, cycling through, to facilitate whatever understanding was needed.

When I first laid them out in a wheel on the floor, they landed much as you see here. I only switched two of them. I didn't think them out or create the orientation; it really felt that they did it themselves.

One of the first things I realized was that neighboring Mothers were similar to each other in certain ways. That is, they share some characteristics with the Mothers next to them. The reason I mention this is that it's important not to get overly hung up on what characteristic belongs to which Mother. They are not mutually exclusive. They're more like watercolors, they blend from one into the next.

When I work Landscape of Mothers as a wheel, I begin at the center with Sun and Moon Mother. She is the one who holds and influences all of the other Landscapes. She is also the one who helps us figure out what the little things are that keep us anchored in our lives. She is our systems, our rituals, our tiny anchors in our every day. Without her in place, the other Mothers become uprooted and may be more likely to express their struggles than their strengths.

THE WHEEL PROCESS

Sun and Moon Mother. We begin at Sun and Moon Mother, acknowledging and tending to our own needs. It helps us be more stable and reliable in our tending to the others in our family, friend group, work group, community, etc. We have the opportunity to really be "in it" together when we know what grounds us. The ability to care for our own nervous system also helps to ground whoever we're with. We learn to co-regulate. We learn to be together and feel rooted, so we feel safer and we can care for each other. We weave together a sense of self and a sense of community.

We can do it when we're dysregulated, which many of us are much of the time. But when we co-regulate there's less drama, less difficulty, and more harmony and understanding. This comes from having our own sense of rhythm and rooting. Co-regulation is a way of interacting with presence. It supports our own nervous system settling, and it is a foundation for shared behaviors and rituals that we do together.

Wind Mother. I start the wheel here, because once we're able to see what our rhythms are and get ourselves settled in them, the next question to ask is "Where do you want to go?" Wind Mother does that. She lifts us up and out of where we are and opens up possibilities. In following Sun and Moon Mother, Wind Mother moves toward new opportunities from a place of self-orientation, rather than from the suggestion or obligation of someone else.

Desert Mother. After Wind Mother, moving clockwise, we meet Desert Mother. She asks us to consider what our boundaries are, and how finding the edges of this new possibility might serve us well.

Island Mother. With Island Mother we contemplate how all of this fits into our value system. Who do we need to be in order to carry this forward?

Mountain Mother. Mountain Mother asks us to find out how we might take a stand. What does this new perspective need? What needs to be done to support it?

River Mother. Next, River Mother aligns our purpose and direction with this new way. Is it a good fit? How does it interact with and support our existing needs and self?

Forest Mother. Forest Mother checks us. She reminds us that whatever we are doing does not only influence us, but others in our lives. Forest Mother asks how our actions contribute to something larger than just us.

Ocean Mother. This is where integration happens. Ocean Mother receives the input of our work. She holds and nourishes it, and she invites us to rest with what we've done. She and Sun and Moon Mother do the weaving while we are still and reflective. And then another question arises and off we go again.

ADDITIONAL THOUGHTS
ABOUT THE WHEEL PROCESS

Start anywhere. Like I said before, you don't have to use it this way; it just makes sense to me to begin with what is new with Wind Mother. So, this is most often how I work with the wheel. The challenge (because there always is one... right?) is that the sequence of Wind Mother, Desert Mother and Island Mother can be a long journey of individuality, introspection, and claiming the Self, and they may be prone to over-thinking. It's a bit of a head-leaning section. It doesn't have to be. Not everyone will see it that way, I imagine, but I feel it. It's a long road to Mountain Mother where you touch back in with something that feels more rooted and stable. So feel free to move from Sun and Moon Mother to any Mother on the wheel.

A strong way to choose where to go from Sun and Moon Mother, if you don't want to engage Wind Mother next, would be to look for a Mother that feels supportive and gentle. For example, if you like the settling aspect of Sun and Moon Mother, you might go from there to Mountain Mother for a deepening of roots and resting into your solidity. Or you might choose to explore Island Mother because you feel uncertain about how to parent from your internal guidance system. It matters less where you start and more that you complete the wheel. The strengths of the Mothers create feedback loops, reinforcing one another as you go.

Coming back to Sun and Moon Mother. Sun and Moon Mother is in the middle because she is so inherently tied to all of the other Mothers. That makes her available at any time. In fact, I feel like she's the "default setting." When everything feels upside down, go back to Sun and Moon and reset the rhythms. Get back in touch with the little things that give you room to take a deep breath.

The Mothers are helpers and guides. To use Landscape of Mothers as a wheel is to give yourself a chance to get to know each of them in turn, not just the one you find "happiest" or the one that looks like a "good mother" or the one you struggle with most. Working with the Landscape of Mothers wheel is a chance to become more evenly versed, more knowledgeable and introspective about each Mother. It is a chance to know yourself better, and to develop the skills and orientations that each Mother provides.

Landscape of Mothers is a little like trying on a new coat. It's an opportunity to try on perspectives as possibilities, explore what it might be like, and make an educated guess about how it'll work for you. In this way it is possible to build the parenting toolbox for the parent you want to be, not who anyone else told you to be.

Getting to know each Mother is also an opportunity to balance between focusing on what is wrong and fixing it, and settling into the celebration of what does work well. Sometimes I find that it's a good choice to build on what works rather than trying to deconstruct what doesn't work. Making something obsolete is as good a strategy as actively tearing it down, but it takes way less effort. Different challenges require different strategies.

Does that mean you'll be an "expert" at the end? No. This is a journey that never ends (sorry). It doesn't mean that Landscape of Mothers has all of your answers. But it is a solid map, and it's been my map for learning who I am and want to be as a mother. It's a map of exploration rather than to an endpoint. I hope it aids in your exploration, and serves as a template for you to draw your own true map.

INSTRUCTIONS FOR THE WHEEL

This is where we put Landscape of Mothers into action. I can provide the map, but you're going to do the work of discerning how much, and which parts of it, look like your inner landscape.

It's totally okay for you to feel that a certain characteristic belongs to a different mother than presented. It's fine if you feel a landscape is missing and you can name it and place it on the wheel. That's how you're going to get to know your map.

What I'm offering is, "Oh, you didn't get a map? Me neither. I made this one for me. How does looking at mine help you find yours?" I'm offering to walk shoulder to shoulder with you, because it took me a rreeaalllyyy long time to map my own inner world.

I'd love it if somehow the part of navigating motherhood where we had to raise ourselves in the midst of the fray became less hard, less isolating, less tumultuous. Let's do this together.

So, let's get to it. It's time for the rubber to meet the road.

As an exploration practice, I invite you to commit to a week with each Mother. At this pace you will get a chance to get to know each Mother, and it won't take too long to get a feeling for them all as a group. If you feel drawn to giving each Mother longer than a week, feel free to do so.

Mother of the Week:

1. Intend to notice thoughts, situations, or people in your life that fall into the realm of that particular Mother. This can be deceptively simple. One of the most common pieces of feedback I've had from people working with Landscape of Mothers is that intention and awareness is a powerful (and easy) step with these archetypes. Don't underestimate what can arise by intentionally choosing your perspective.

2. Read through the description of the Landscape Mother you are working with this week. Don't think too hard about it. Just let the imagery and concepts settle in you. I consider this to be an open ended-question for the brain. Basically, we are saying "what in my life is like this?"

3. Sometime during the week, make time to sit down and move the feelings you have into words. You can do this through answering the questions on the next page, or you can write freeform in a journal of your choice. If you're using the questions provided, I recommend making copies of the page, or transcribing them to a place where you can reference them easily.

Questions for working with the Mothers as a Wheel

Name of the Mother you are reflecting on:

How do I express the strengths of this Mother in my daily life?

What expressions of the strengths feel like they are correct? Which ones need to change?

How do I express the struggles of this Mother in my daily life?

What expressions of the struggles feel like they are the most difficult?

How could I utilize the strengths of this Mother to help me with my struggles?

To what tangible tasks or activities can I commit, so that I can make sure I am taking care of myself?

Is there any insight from neighboring Mothers on the wheel? Do their strengths apply here? Does their expression of the struggle help me understand what's happening for me?

Landscape of Mothers is an ongoing process of locating ourselves when we feel lost or uncertain, connecting back to our guidance and choice, and stepping into the journey again. It is not a definitive answer, a mastery program, or a completion of some particular life phase. It is the stuff of the everyday. It is a way to pull things apart a bit, to find space for finding one's own path, and to step into our autonomy and choice.

Underneath the individual work, Landscape of Mothers invites you into a deeper movement—away from the expectations, roles, demands, institutions, and processes of our culture, and into feeling your own way through the world in accordance with your values and vision. It steps out of dualistic and restrictive ways that pigeonhole people into feeling that they have no choices.

Landscape of Mothers has the potential to be a map of liberation: for you personally, and for all of us if we do it together. While this is the big vision I have for Landscape of Mothers, I also know that it all begins with our own internal freedom to choose our legacy. My desired legacy is one of interconnectedness, cherished individuality, and recognizing that our most precious resource is one another.

May we all hold ourselves tenderly, may we view others with compassion and curiosity, and may we collectively hone our strength and courage for equity and caring.

Thank you for being on this journey with me.

ACKNOWLEDGMENTS

I want to thank those whose work taught and inspired me, and kept me going with my own healing journey. I didn't do any of this alone. You provided understanding and foundation for me to take on the job of healing myself from my harmful ancestral patterns so that I could do something different for my children.

I'm grateful for bodies of work that changed the way I thought about myself, particularly John Bowlby's Theory of Attachment, and John Gottman's popularization and explanation of that theory as it relates to adult human relationships. Thanks to Peter Levine for his work on Somatic Experiencing as a way to work through trauma and stress in the body.

The book that catalyzed my process and began to put words to so much of my experience was Harriet Lerner's *The Mother Dance: How Children Change Your Life*. The relief of having the words for what was happening in me and my family, and the heartbreak of seeing it in print, together made room for change.

For decades I have traveled with Women Who Run With The Wolves. Thank you to Clarisa Pinkola Estés for her brilliance around storytelling, empowerment, and shedding the things that hold us back.

Deep forever thanks to Nina Simons, Rachel Bagby, and Tobi Herzlich and the Spring 2017 cohort of Cultivating Women's Leadership. You helped me see how important this project was and why I might want to share it with others. Thank you for your guidance, encouragement, and insight.

Thank you Pixie Lighthorse for deepening my understanding of how to interpret the natural world through metaphor and observation. Through earth medicine I came to understand how nature could provide me with intentional healing.

To Jen Lemen and her work, The Path of Devotion, and the people who gather there, all of whom helped (and continue to help) me understand belonging, togetherness, and the power of the small things to make a big difference. Jen also showed me how systems can cause harm, shifting my perspective about responsibility and the capacity for amends.

And to Greg Booi for the ongoing shop talk and early enthusiasm for this work. You were the first to notice the parallels between the stories I was telling and the underlying pillars of healing. Thank you for pointing that out, as it made all the difference!

Sirena Andrea, thank you for so many opportunities to share stories with you. I'll never get enough of it. The roots of Landscape of Mothers lie in our early days of storytelling, and exploring archetype and metaphor with you has been nothing short of exquisite.

In what feels like "the way-back-days," Renee Tennant introduced me to a whole world of energy and choice and power when I felt like I had none. Priscilla Kapel stood for my healing over my academic education when things were getting down to critical decision time. And to the Bioenergy Balancing community that will always be my mentors... thank you all.

And in even further back days, thank you to Kate McCarthy Healy for introducing me to the concept that nature could hold and be the source of my spirituality.

Special blessings to the preschool teachers at Santa Cruz Parent Education Nursery School who held me when times were hard and I was struggling as a new parent. Wendy Wyckoff, Maggie Klepp, and Dara Thornton. You asked the "just right" questions with such tenderness. I appreciate you more than you know.

To my teachers and mentors in Conservation Biology, this is what came out of all of my work in the field and the PhD process. I know it isn't what any of us expected. The time I spent immersing myself in the ecology of places let me better understand what I learned in the classroom, and being in your labs supported me to think creatively. Thank you especially to Paul Beier and Thomas Sisk at Northern Arizona University.

Nothing like this happens without so many people gathering to encourage and support. Deep thanks to my Book Witch, Heather Dakota, without whom this book would have never made it to print. Her encouragement in the early days and masterful skills are everything. Thank you Heather!

To my beta readers and friends who gathered for early drafts, your insights and thoughtfulness were beyond anything I could have ever imagined. Your work made this work better! Overwhelming gratitude to The Explorer's Club: Nancy Voogd, Erin McDermott, Julia Ferguson Andriessen, and Julia Thompson. Thank you to my beta readers: Edwina Clarke, Mischa Revotskie, Catherine Beerda-Basso, and Kieran McDermott.

Thanks to Michael Clifton, without you this project would have never come to fruition. And thank you most of all for learning along with me.

Last, but not least, thank you to Phoebe Clifton, Nora Clifton, and Emily Nason. You are the flesh and blood that have carried me through this project. May you be held, may you be certain that you are loved, and may you know happiness always.

ABOUT JILL DONEEN CLIFTON

Jill Doneen Clifton is a writer, facilitator, and student of nature. She uses nature and archetypes to help guide moms through the lingering effects of childhood experiences to become the kind of parents they want to be.

Originally trained as a biologist, Jill weaves her coaching with nature-based practices. *Landscape of Mothers* is her deep belief that being together can create resilience in times of uncertainty and change. She lives with her family in Northern California, near the *Ocean Mother.*

Learn more about Landscape of Mothers *at*
www.landscapeofmothers.com